Prehistoric and
Viking Shetland

Prehistoric and Viking Shetland

Noel Fojut

Published by
The Shetland Times Ltd.,
Lerwick, Shetland.

A CIP catalogue record for this book is available from the British Library.

ISBN 1 904746 07 1
ISBN 978 1 904746 07 2

First edition 1981.
Second edition 1986.
Third edition 1994.
Fourth edition 1994.

Cover photograph:
Troswick, standing stone, Dunrossness.

Printed and published by
The Shetland Times Ltd., Gremista, Lerwick,
Shetland, ZE1 0PX, Scotland

Contents

Introduction and Acknowledgements

DESCRIBING the period from the earliest human presence in Shetland up to the period of the Norse settlement, this guide draws on the field evidence of archaeological remains, on the results of many surveys, excavations and scientific studies, and on museum collections of artefacts. The recent discovery of evidence for pre-farming settlement means this period now spans well over six thousand years. Such a stretch of time cannot be covered in detail in so small a space. Instead, the intention here is to provide a guide for Shetlanders and visitors who want to know about the archaeology of the Islands, and an introduction to Shetland for archaeologists.

The main section of this guide is a description and discussion of what archaeology can tell us about Shetland's past. Rather than a strict century-by-century account, this is constructed as a series of nine extended essays, in roughly chronological order, each dwelling upon a particular theme or period. This narrative section is followed by a gazetteer of some of the best and most accessible sites, enough to keep an energetic visitor busy for several weeks. The guide closes with a series of suggested tours, taking in a good range of these sites in reasonably short day trips.

This guide carries the warning that many of its statements about how things were in past times are not proven facts, but only my interpretations of the evidence. Others might offer very different views. There is still relatively little data, and much of what exists remains poorly understood. There are yawning gaps, whole centuries for which there is no firmly dated information, so many generalisations are made here on the flimsiest of evidence, sometimes by analogy and sometimes upon intuition alone. Hopefully, readers will look for themselves at the evidence of Shetland's ancient sites and landscapes, read the excavation reports, study the survey maps and think about what they see, going on to develop a deeper understanding of society in those remote times.

This is only the merest skeleton of what archaeologists have established. Even fully fleshed, however, the body of knowledge remains a slender one. But, like the author, it grows steadily more rounded as each year passes. This new edition presents fresh evidence about the earliest settlement of Shetland. It offers fresh perspectives derived from recent surveys, excavations and conferences on all periods, but in particular takes a new look at the middle and later Iron Age, a time when Shetland experienced social change of a scale and rapidity unmatched until the modern era. There is enough new material presented here that those who own earlier editions may find it worth at least borrowing this new one, to see how knowledge has progressed and how far old theories have been recanted upon.

Like all guides, this is a synthesis built by ruthlessly exploiting others' labours. Its compilation and successive revisions have created a huge and un-repayable debt to many Shetlanders and fellow archaeologists, but most of all to the small but increasing number who are both. Shetland's official Archaeologist, Val Turner, has given

Introduction and Acknowledgements

hugely of her time, knowledge and friendship since her appointment in 1987, as have her colleagues at the Shetland Amenity Trust. The staff of the Shetland Museum, under its successive curators, Tom Henderson, Andrew Williamson and Tommy Watt, have helped with matters artefactual, social and much more besides. Shetland's Archivist, Brian Smith, has performed the difficult task of keeping my feet firmly in the realities of Shetland, while at the same time, through his own research collaboration with Gordon Johnston, stimulating some radical thinking about Iron Age society.

For discussions, on-site and off, and generous permission to draw on published and unpublished results of projects past and current, thanks are due to many excavators and surveyors. They are not named individually here, for fear of accidentally omitting one. Colleagues past and present at Historic Scotland have encouraged my Shetland obsession over three decades. Daniel Thérond of the Council of Europe kindly permitted Shetland's annexation of desk and computer from time to time during my secondment to Strasbourg in 2004-5. Fiona Stewart, my long-suffering wife, expert typist and proof-reader, helped tremendously in preparing the revised text.

Everyone mentioned above will be relieved to learn that while I gratefully acknowledge their inspiration and help, I accept full responsibility for ideas as they are expressed in this book – especially those ideas which have been transformed markedly since first expressed by their proponents.

No one can conduct worthwhile research in Shetland (or anywhere else) without the contribution of countless and often anonymous local people. Since 1976, Shetlanders have been offering me directions, more or less accurately, in search of "lumps, bumps and old stones". The people of Shetland have long taken their history and archaeology – and visiting historians and archaeologists – to their hearts. They politely subject our more outlandish theories to the test of common sense and provide essential support which, in my case, has ranged from companionship, information and advice to the provision of boats, hot baths, breakdown services and, last but not least, regular and copious supplies of tea and home-bakes.

This new edition is dedicated to my mother, Honour Fojut, who encouraged my early interest in things natural, geographical, geological and archaeological, and who patiently supported me through changing enthusiasms and career diversions. I hope it compensates in some small measure for the occasions when mothers of my former schoolmates have asked her if her son was still in archaeology, or whether he had finally "got a proper job".

Noel Fojut
Strasbourg and Edinburgh,
2005-2006

2

CLIMATE, geology and geography combine to give Shetland a distinctive natural environment, one with many features which are unique in Britain. From the viewpoint of human settlement, the islands have been habitable since the end of the last Ice Age, although sometimes only marginally so. The physical background to Shetland's prehistory and history, and to present day life there, can never be ignored. Even in today's advanced technological world, climate and weather are in the forefront of every Shetlander's mind. How much more so in the past, in the days before waterproof clothing, electric heating, safe transport and imported food?

The island chain lies at the junction of the North Sea and the Atlantic Ocean, near the edge of the European continental shelf. Its oceanic climate banishes long winter frosts but also keeps summer temperatures moderate. In a regime of adequate but not excessive rainfall with equable temperatures, the long summer days granted by Shetland's relatively northern location allow a few crops to be raised over a short growing period. Conversely, the short winter days make for a lengthy dead season.

The main obstacle to farming is the wind, for Shetland at sea level is the windiest area of Britain. The wind inhibits growth both by its own force and by the fact that it carries a heavy load of fine salt particles, picked up from spray breaking over the many coastal skerries and cliffs. Where the salt load is strongest, along exposed cliff tops, nothing grows but a mat of sea-pink and wiry grass, while even

inland the wind's influence is never absent, leading to the abundance of drystone dykes (walls) so typical of rural Shetland. These serve as much as windbreaks as field boundaries. On the highest summits, wind exposure and winter frosts maintain habitats of stunted arctic-alpine vegetation which delight botanists and serve as a reminder of just how close Shetland is to the Arctic.

The land-mass of Shetland consists of the upper portions of a semi-submerged chain of hills. In broad outline Shetland retains an essentially pre-glacial landscape, parallel ridges of rock running north-south having been accentuated by millions of years of erosion into a landscape of long, whale-backed hills with narrow valleys between. Although clay, sand and gravel were extensively deposited during the Ice Age, giving much of the land a poorly developed drainage system, and despite the glacial erosion which has steepened some coastal cliffs, these were relatively small-scale modifications to the overall pre-glacial shape of the land.

Erratics are spectacular evidence of glacial action – Out Skerries.

3

This aerial view of Banna Minn, West Burra, shows the different elements of "typical" Shetland coastline, with the open sea towards the foot of the picture (west), a bay with sand and shingle beaches and a long sheltered inlet behind.

Land and water are inextricably entangled, for not only do elongated drowned valleys reach deep into the interior, but the whole surface is scattered with thousands of small lochs, marshes and streams, so that a cross-country journey which seems short on the map may in reality become quite a major undertaking. This interpenetration of land and water, combined with the fact that the land is split up into fragments – at least 500 larger and smaller islands, islets and rocks, of which only 16 are permanently inhabited today – has led to the lifestyle which has made the typical Shetlander "a fisherman with a croft" as opposed to "a crofter with a boat" as is said of neighbouring Orcadians. Only in recent years has the sea ceased to be the main medium of transport: in 1793 a former resident of Nesting could say that "the roads, bridges etc., are in the same state here as in every other part of Shetland, that is to say, there are none".

The sea, having brought the first and subsequent settlers, has provided much-needed security of food supply and has made survival possible in the all too frequent years when late springs, wet summers and tempestuous autumns have meant poor or non-existent harvests. Of course, fish were once much more abundant than they are today, both inshore and in deeper waters, while whales, seals, otters, seabirds and wildfowl have been exploited, often at great risk, from the earliest days. More static resources, such as the eggs of seabirds, shellfish, seaweed and algae were often an essential part of the daily diet, rather than an occasional extra.

Behind the seashore lies the land. Mostly this is a rock-strewn landscape of heather and sedge, often growing over deep peat, broken in places by signs of long human perseverance in the form of the green patches of improved pasture or former cropland. Except in a few favoured areas, tilled fields are small, poor and prone to waterlogging. Formerly, much more land was cultivated, and traces of earlier agriculture are everywhere: indeed, as will be seen, the long-term history of farming in Shetland represents a steady decline in the extent of arable cultivation from the earliest days towards the present time.

Small bands of limestone have provided the most fertile soils, while localised areas of sand accumulation behind beaches have allowed some extensive agriculture. On the sandy areas and elsewhere, natural soils have been improved over the centuries by the addition of organic material – animal manure, rotted seaweed, decayed thatch and household waste. It would be fair to say that any smooth green field in Shetland equates to many lifetimes of back-breaking labour.

The higher ridges, hills and moors generally lie under a desolate blanket of peat, formed by centuries of accumulating vegetation debris. Trees are few and treasured, but occasional clumps of scrub willow and birch on isolated holms and inaccessible cliffs, together with a handful of hazel and aspen bushes, point to a past landscape which was, if not heavily forested, at least more well-wooded than today. Substantial thicknesses of timber are sometimes encountered in cutting peat for domestic fuel. Scientific studies into the past vegetation cover, based on the remains of plants and on pollen recovered in cores taken from peat

bogs and lake sediments, have confirmed that the present treeless state of Shetland is not original. It arises from a combination of grazing by livestock (who find tree seedlings tasty), climatic change (which has created waterlogged ground conditions where tree seeds will not germinate or establish roots) and soil deterioration (which has reduced the nutrient status of soils, preventing or stunting growth even if a seedling does get a start). All of the taller trees in the islands today have been planted and carefully protected.

In prehistoric times driftwood seems to have been used in great quantities, suggesting that even then Shetland's trees, while more numerous, were generally not of great size, probably growing as a low, but dense scrub woodland. To picture the landscape before man came upon the scene, one might call to mind the old Icelandic joke: "Question: What should one do if lost in a forest in Iceland? Answer: Stand up!"

How Shetland may have looked at its most wooded, 6000-5000 BC. (The photograph was taken near Callander in Stirlingshire.)

Shingle pits and beaches form in sheltered bays and inlets – Dales Voe.

Cliffs defend the "outer coast" – Reeva, Fair Isle.

The coastal fringe merits a closer examination, for it has been here, where the farms meet the fishing grounds, that most of Shetland life has always been lived. Along with the west coast of the Outer Hebrides, Shetland is unusual in northern Britain in having a coastline which is slowly sinking, rather than

rising. During the Ice Age, the great weight of ice over Scotland pressed down the central landmass, raising the outer periphery. Now that the ice has melted, the land is still regaining its equilibrium, and the central areas of Scotland are rising while the edges sink. It has been estimated that Shetland sank, on average, two metres per thousand years for several millennia after the Ice Age, slowing down to less than one metre per millennium from about 1000 BC onwards. Today it is hard to separate the residual effects of post-glacial sinkage from the effects of globally-rising sea-level.

The effects of rising sea-levels on the form of the coastline vary greatly. On the outer coasts, some pre-existing cliffs were freshened up by the passage of ice, and in places these are now being actively eroded by the sea: the south end of Bressay is a good example. However, most cliffs are fairly stable, as witness the grassed-over boulders lying at the foot of headlands such as Herma Ness. Behind the cliffed outer ramparts lie two main types of shoreline. The first is a series of low, rocky slopes broken by small bays, typified by the shores of Sandness and Nesting. The second is the more hospitable coastline found along the long inlets, or voes, drowned valleys where storm waves lose their force to break on gentle slopes which run down to the sea.

The slow sinking of the land, combined with past erosion by ice, has provided a plentiful supply of sand and shingle offshore, which wave action has built up into a fine array of beaches, some of curious form, such as the multiple bay-head and bay-mouth bars in Dales Voe, or

the tombolo (double back-to-back beach) which links St Ninian's Isle to the shore below Bigton. As the land sinks, such beaches adapt themselves to new sea levels, growing slowly by natural accretion – unless the equilibrium is disturbed by human activity.

Behind some of the larger beaches, great spreads of sand have been blown inland to be trapped and stabilised by the roots of coarse grasses. Such areas are well-drained and fertile – in Gaelic-speaking parts (which Shetland is not) these sand-plains would be called *machair*. These light soils have long been cultivated but are always prone to erosion when their seaward slopes are broken by over-grazing or careless removal of sand for construction or agriculture. Areas around Scatness, Jarlshof and Quendale in the south, and Breakon in Yell, have suffered repeatedly from sand-blows, which can be severe enough to sterilise large extents of arable land and even to bury houses. But the attractiveness of such areas for settlement is shown by the constant renewal of half-buried villages at Jarlshof. From early times, Shetlanders must have had to become hardened to occasional disasters in their bid to carve out a living from the land.

Despite the first impression of rugged cliffs and barren moors, the true Shetland, that of the people, is this gentler coast around the sheltered voes, where long-worked fields run down to small strips of shingle beach where boats can be drawn up above the waves. On shores such as these are found the first traces of human presence in Shetland – explorers beginning a six-thousand year struggle against wind and wave, seeking a living along the tide-line and among scrub-covered hills, at the end of the settled world.

Sandy beaches are relatively scarce – Papil, Fetlar.

7

Early Explorers

UNTIL a few years ago, the archaeology of Shetland began with the arrival of the first farmers, some time well before 3000 BC, but certainly after 4000 BC. But the recent discovery of a site at West of Voe of Sumburgh has pushed that date back by at least a thousand years, and seems to be confirming hints from analysis of past vegetation patterns that the human presence in Shetland began earlier than previously thought.

Previously, the accepted wisdom was that Shetland might have been visited at an early date by people living a hunting, fishing and gathering lifestyle – of the type archaeologists call "Mesolithic" –

Coastal erosion continues to reveal many archaeological sites.

but that such visitors had not settled. The argument went thus: because Shetland was separated from Orkney by a deep and wide sea passage from the end of the Ice Age onwards, there was no land bridge for sizeable land mammals to cross into the islands, and this lack meant the standard Mesolithic economy, which was understood as based largely on hunting, was not viable. In any case, it was thought that the remains of any encampments or settlements from short-lived forays would have been situated close beside the shore and would probably have been lost to rising sea-level. As a result, earlier editions of this guide concluded that the question of pre-agricultural settlement "may never be resolved".

Publishing such a conclusion almost seems to invite contradiction. The first possible evidence for a human presence in Shetland before the mid 3000s BC was noted in the 1990s, not by archaeologists but by palaeo-botanists. It took the form of a distinct drop in the pollen levels from scrub woodland and an increase in the pollen of plant species associated with open ground. Although climate change alone might have produced this effect, those who identified this evidence at a small number of localities tentatively suggested that the change could be associated with grazing by deliberately introduced grazing animals – which at this date would have been red deer – as early as 5500 BC. There is good evidence from elsewhere in north west Europe that Mesolithic communities manipulated forest cover, often using fire, to create clearings into which deer could be hunted and to

which they would be drawn by fresh young growth. In some parts of Europe, red deer seem to have become semi-domesticated as a result.

However, the complete absence of any of the typical Mesolithic flint artefacts or dated settlement sites in Shetland – with the exception of a solitary flint axe found many years ago in Fair Isle – and the seeming implausibility of such early visitors having boats capable of open-sea transport of deer in numbers sufficient to set up a breeding population, led to a reluctance to accept this daring interpretation. Also, the fact that woodland cover subsequently regained its former extent, implying that the hypothetical deer had died out, added another strand to the complicated nature of this theory,

which was at best regarded as "interesting".

Then, in 2002, a radiocarbon date of around 4200 BC was obtained from oyster shells in an eroding midden (rubbish heap) associated with a possible settlement site just above the shore at West Voe of Sumburgh, near the southern tip of the islands. The pessimists had been proved wrong, and Shetland had its first – and so far only – Mesolithic site. Its exploration is continuing.

Apart from the fact that one group visited Shetland and stayed long enough to build up a small rubbish heap of shellfish remains, with fragments of seal and whale bone, we still know next to nothing about pre-agricultural Shetland, but we can make some deductions. It seems reasonable to assume that this site, at the south end of the islands, was

The West Voe of Sumburgh – where the first Shetlanders may have landed, although rising sea-levels mean the coastline has changed greatly since then.

not unique, and also that those who used it would have explored widely and, if they were not permanent settlers, they would certainly have been regular visitors. Either way, they clearly possessed boats adequate enough to make the exposed sea crossing, most likely from Orkney via Fair Isle, with a reasonable expectation of arriving and returning alive. Although the climate then was better, and perhaps less stormy, there is no doubt that the crossing would have been a daunting prospect then as now, with awkward currents and uncomfortable seas, even in calm weather.

Old boats have other uses – this modern example at Norwick, Unst, reflects an age-old practice.

Whether or not the first arrivals did introduce red deer (a small number of pregnant does or a collection of just-weaned calves would have been the most economical way of starting a breeding population), they almost certainly would have brought dogs – the earliest domesticated animal. Perhaps they accidentally introduced shrews and mice, so bringing about lasting changes to the natural environment. One change that certainly happened at Sumburgh, some time over the following 1500 years, was the local extinction of oysters: by the time of the earliest deposits at nearby Jarlshof the abundant shell middens there include no oysters. Whether the demise of the Sumburgh oysters was due to over-exploitation or simply to some natural change of climate or sea-bed conditions remains unclear.

The Sumburgh area is where one might expect to find the earliest arrivals – it is, after all, the first landfall for boats coming from the south – but given that the lifestyle of the period was a semi-nomadic one, following animals, searching for edible plants but above all dependent upon fishing and gathering shellfish, it seems reasonable to assume that the coastline and valleys of Shetland were thoroughly explored soon after the first people arrived. In the minds and traditions of these settlers a comprehensive map of all the resources relevant to their survival would have quickly built up – food supplies, shelters, tides, currents, sources of water and of fuel.

For the time being, that is as much as can be said about Shetland's archaeology before the first farmers.

However, it is in the nature of archaeology that once a type of site or other form of evidence is known to exist in an area, more are soon discovered. In recent years sites of the Mesolithic period have been successively located in almost every part of Scotland from which they were formerly unknown. Ironically, the sole exception is Orkney. However, now that Shetland has evidence for the Mesolithic period, this has raised the hopes of Orkney-based researchers. Certainly it seems unlikely that the first settlers of Shetland would have accidentally or deliberately bypassed Orkney.

Shetland was now integrated as part of the human world for the first time since the Ice Age. The sea route was established and would not be forgotten. The inhabitants of Orkney, and northern Scotland in general, now knew that the little dots on the far horizon, visible from hills in the north of Orkney, marked a substantial group of islands rich in fish and shellfish, seabirds and marine mammals. And soon, quite possibly, they would have had relatives or former neighbours living there.

It is generally believed that line-of-sight was vital to early navigators (although evidence for the early settlement of Australia has recently called this into question). Following the land north, Orkney can be seen from the Scottish mainland, the tall islands of Fair Isle and Foula can be seen from Orkney and from these Shetland's main island (confusingly, for southerners, called "Mainland") is visible. From Mainland all the other Shetland isles are in view, up to Unst. Off Unst's northern tip lie the rocks of Muckle Flugga, beyond which there is no further land in line-of-sight. It may not be coincidental that all the evidence (so far) suggests that the next island group to the north west, the Faeroes, were not to be settled until nearly 5000 years later. For all of that period, Shetland was, literally, regarded as the end of the world.

Will we ever find the home of the very first Shetlanders? Given our rather haphazard investigations, it would be quite surprising if we did, indeed, find the earliest settlement site. First, the very earliest site may already have been destroyed by natural erosion or some building project in years gone by. Second, even finding the oldest surviving site is beyond us: we might already have found it, but not have recognised it, perhaps for lack of reliable dating evidence. Further, even if we dug every promising site, we might miss the earliest one, because it might be somewhere we did not, or could not, look: below an inhabited home, or in some bizarre and unexpected location. Even given infinite resources, we could excavate every square metre of the islands and still not solve this particular puzzle.

So archaeologists can only offer "the earliest settlement so far reliably dated". The nature of our techniques and way in which evidence survives mean that, in archaeology as in the world of sporting prowess, there is no absolute limit to what may be achieved and always the chance of yet another "best so far". It helps to keep us digging.

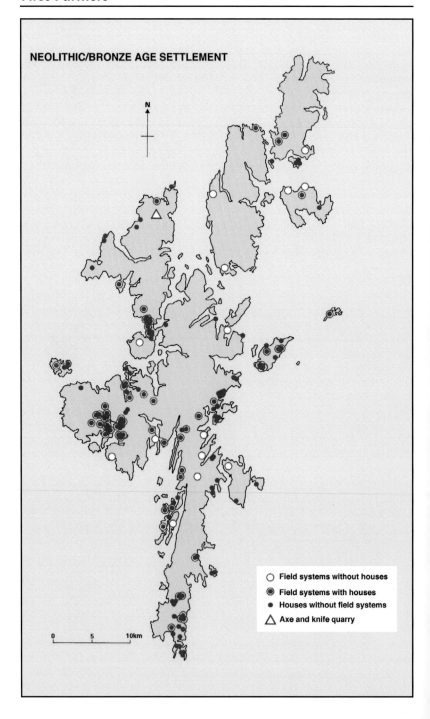

APART from these tantalising traces of the earliest Shetlanders, the next solid evidence begins to appear much later, in the few centuries just before 3000 BC. By this time, early farmers, with the combination of characteristics termed Neolithic, were well established all over Shetland. We do not know when farming began in Shetland, or whether it was introduced by a new group of people or by the descendants of the Mesolithic communities who had hunted and fished around Shetland for many generations. Archaeologists used to explain every change by "invasions", but in recent years "gradual adaptation" has been more fashionable. In Shetland there is some evidence which suggests, if not an invasion, at least a rapid expansion of population when farming became established. But there are also some features which might best be explained if farming had been adopted by a people who were already long-established.

The earliest dates from Neolithic sites are around 3200 BC, for two very different sites. One is a multiple burial in a stone-built coffin, or cist, found at Sumburgh airport. Burial implies people to die and people to bury the dead, while anything other than a hole in the ground implies a belief system in which the remains of the dead are of some importance. The other site is on Ward of Shurton, a hill to the south-east of Lerwick, where the building of a boundary dyke (in Shetland, dykes are walls, not ditches as some other parts of Europe) has been given a similar date. Such a wall would be an unlikely first construction project for people in a country with no natural predators or competitors. Both sites therefore imply that by this date a relatively sophisticated people with religious beliefs and an eye to territorial demarcation had set up home in Shetland. These are both characteristics which are normally associated with the "Neolithic farming revolution", and fragments of a large pottery vessel found in the grave at Sumburgh would also fit this assertion.

The 1970s' excavations at Scord of Brouster, near Bridge of Walls in the West Mainland, suggested a similar date for a slight wooden construction, perhaps a house, underlying a later stone-built dwelling. More importantly, this site is one of several to produce direct evidence for agriculture, in the form of discarded stone plough-shares and mattocks and also characteristic grooves in the subsoil formed by the use of such primitive implements. This evidence for agriculture is important, because it demonstrates the inhabitants were practising the "full Neolithic package" of farming, and not just Mesolithic hunter-gatherers who had decided to build substantial houses modelled on those of farming neighbours elsewhere.

It is interesting that, by the time we have evidence for the Neolithic life styles in Shetland, some aspects have already developed differences from that of Orkney or of the Hebrides. The pottery is clearly related to that found in Orkney at slightly later sites such as Rinyo, Skara Brae and Barnhouse, but has its own distinctive style. The earliest pottery of all so far, that from the Sumburgh cist burial, is more Hebridean than Orcadian in style.

A small oval prehistoric house built alongside an earlier "perched block" wall – Gorda Water, Papa Stour.

The stone-built houses of this period are clearly of the same general family as those at Orkney sites like Skara Brae, but once again they are distinctive, being oval, rather than sub-rectangular. Doubtless building styles had much to do with the geology of the islands, but it would still have required time to develop styles which reflected the local materials.

These observations point to the Shetland Neolithic being established some centuries before our earliest dated sites – hence the suggestion of 3500 BC as a possible date for the start of this period in Shetland. By the time of our earliest surviving evidence, Neolithic Shetlanders had already developed a distinctive culture and no doubt the independent character which has marked them ever since.

The ideas of farming, if not the farmers themselves, came from the

south. Farming was well-established along the banks of the River Dee in Aberdeenshire soon after 4000 BC, from which it probably spread to Orkney not long after. Shetland would not have been far behind. We do not know if the ideas arrived one-by-one, or as a complete package. But within a few centuries, domesticated animals, arable crops, the tools needed to farm them and process their various products and the necessary skills and knowledge had all arrived.

These early farming communities seem to have been family-sized groups, each practising mixed agriculture on an individual farm spread around a single dwelling. The main crop was barley. (Wheat was known at this period, and cultivated as far north as Aberdeenshire, but even allowing for the climate being milder then than now, Shetland was a little too far north.) This early barley was of a type akin to medieval bere. Oats seem not to have been grown until much later. Cultivation tools – wooden implements including stone-bladed mattocks and simple ploughs with stone tips – must have arrived at the same time as the crops. Food plants such as sorrel and goosefoot, whose leaves were once simply gathered from the wild, may even have been cultivated on a small scale as vegetables, to add greenstuff to the diet.

Sheep and cattle also arrived early, and their bones have been found on a few sites. Implements for spinning and weaving wool and for dressing skins would have come in as well, the latter developed from those used by earlier hunters. Interestingly the pig seems to have been a late and apparently a rather reluctant arrival. Originally a woodland creature, by the time the pig reached Shetland most of the original tree cover had gone, and the pig seems never to have been quite as much a part of the Shetland farming scene as it was elsewhere in the north. No doubt dogs, already domesticated for hunting, were trained to herd livestock, while many other traces of the old Mesolithic lifestyle may have lingered on.

The modern fashion is for archaeologists to regard this farming assemblage as having been built up piecemeal rather than imported as a complete kit, so we do not need to envisage large vessels arriving on the southern coast laden with seed, implements, livestock and farmers "ready to go", but we can be sure that these early farmers had access to reliable boats, presumably descended from those used for hunting and fishing by their

Stone ard point: tip of a prehistoric stilt plough. Found protruding from the ground surface near the prehistoric houses at Grunnavoe, West Mainland (17).

Mesolithic predecessors. As they steadily adapted to the more sedentary lifestyle associated with farming, they would still have exploited the resources of sea and shore, as Shetlanders have continued to do up to the present day. With a growing population, there might have been some trade between settlements. Old boats might well have been used as roofs for sheds and houses, but there would always have been sufficient vessels in good repair to allow for fishing trips and visits along the coast to neighbours.

Compared with hunting and fishing, farming provides a more steady, reliable, food supply, but the price is a larger investment of labour per unit of nutrition. Agriculture, especially arable, needs a larger labour force, differently organised. Rather than the small, skilled groups required for hunting, which left the younger, older and less able members of each community free to gather static food resources and to process the catch gathered by agile hunters and fishermen, crop-raising absorbs regular inputs of hard labour from almost everyone who can lend a hand. The ploughing and turning over of the soil, the gathering of stones, spreading of manure, weeding, harvesting, drying and

Ancient field walling emerging from below peat at Scord of Wadbister – many remains of prehistoric farming settlement were buried by peat as climate deteriorated during the Bronze Age.

boundaries. If this sequence is correct, it suggests an early concern with land division which might imply that sizeable numbers arrived at more or less the same time. It is not a pattern which would be expected if the settlement of each area began with a single modest farm in an otherwise empty landscape, but more akin to what was done very much later when the Vikings settled into empty Iceland, with the pioneers dividing up the land for the benefit of their families who were following on behind. This idea could be tested quite easily by a small programme of excavating the junctions of these old field walls, to see if indeed the apparent priority of the large cross-country "estate boundary" walls is genuine, or just an illusion because they are more substantial than the sub-dividing walls which seem to run into them.

threshing the grain: the price for security of food supplies is high, especially in a society which was almost entirely un-mechanised, apart from primitive ploughs and perhaps harrows, drawn by cattle or even human traction. Assured food supplies allow populations to grow faster, permitting more land to be cultivated and tending to encourage farming populations to spread out over former hunting areas.

Although we now know that the first farmers were not Shetland's earliest settlers, it does seem that the population increased rapidly when farming became established. This may have been due to a relatively short-lived period of immigration as much as to natural increase of the local population. The reason for this immigration hypothesis is that, where there is the best evidence for early farming settlement, as in the West Mainland, the land seems to have been divided up by substantial walls which run across country for long distances, carving the countryside up into large units which are then subdivided by lesser

Simply being able to consider such a programme of research reminds us that Shetland has some of the best surviving field evidence of early agricultural settlement anywhere in the British Isles. Only Dartmoor and the West Coast of Ireland can compare. Shetland may lack the spectacular set-piece monuments of its neighbour Orkney, but it more than compensates for this by the richness and completeness of its prehistoric archaeology, especially for the Neolithic period.

Why is this preservation so good? Firstly, many buildings and boundaries were of stone, perhaps with a little turf to heighten wall tops. Roofs would have been low-pitched and thatched, using reeds, heather or, once farming was well established, straw. When such structures are abandoned, the stone walls last almost indefinitely unless they are removed. Secondly, something happened to prevent these old structures being removed. Almost as soon as farming was established, the climate began to deteriorate. Summers became cooler and wetter, and winters more stormy. From as early as 2000 BC in some places, and generally from 1000 BC onwards, cultivation of the higher ground became increasingly unviable and fields and farmsteads were abandoned and turned over to sheep or cattle grazing instead. Gradually peat grew over the ruins of abandoned houses and field walls, sealing these remains for centuries to come.

It is no coincidence that the areas which have the best surviving remains of these early farming landscapes are those which have been stripped of peat relatively recently – in the last two centuries or so. Areas worked out long ago seem to have fewer remains of this period. This is almost certainly not because such remains were not there below the peat, but because their stones have been exposed longer and have largely been carted off to use elsewhere. (Recycling may be environmentally sound, but it is not something which delights archaeologists, at least in ancient times.) Fortunately there are still large areas covered by peat, where cutting has not commenced yet, or is still relatively limited in extent. Good examples of recently exposed prehistoric houses can be seen in some of these areas, notably along the roadside leading from Skellister to North Nesting (11). Now that the archaeological importance of these tumbled stones is more widely

appreciated, those cutting peat tend to try to leave them undisturbed, working around them rather than moving them out of their way.

What is perhaps most remarkable of all is that these early sites – and Shetland has more above-ground ruins of pre Iron Age houses than any comparable-sized area in Europe – were not recognised for what they were until the 1940s. Archaeologists were fewer in number in those days. Used to working in more southern parts, early investigators simply refused to believe that the profusion of ruined oval houses littering the landscape could all be early in date, even though they could see that in some places they were clearly earlier than the peat cover. The long-running national survey of Scotland's archaeology, which dealt with Shetland around 1936, noted hardly any of these structures, describing the few it did recognise as "indeterminate structures". But one of the national survey's field officers, Charles Calder, began to realise the potential of the Shetland sites, and undertook excavations at several,

A large oval prehistoric house at Gruting – in the 1940s excavator referred to this site as "Gruting School", but the former side-school has long since closed (19).

including Gruting School (19), Ness of Gruting (20) and Stanydale (18) in the 1940s and early 1950s, convincingly demonstrating that these were, indeed, dwellings of the later Neolithic or early Bronze Age. Although at the time there was no radiocarbon dating to put more exact dates on such sites – pottery and other artefacts provided comparative dates only – we would now date them to the period from just before 3000 BC to as late as 1000 BC.

For the visitor today, the best area in which to see these prehistoric agricultural remains is the West Mainland. From Loch of Grunnavoe north, via Bridge of Walls, Voxterby and Sulma Water to the sea, a distance of 10km, there is always some item of this period on view on the lower slopes, be it burial cairn, field wall or ruined farmhouse. Small mounds of stones cleared from the ploughsoil dot the landscape everywhere, and sometimes close inspection of these will reveal early stone plough-points or rough mattocks, discarded after damage during cultivation. Nor is this the only part of Shetland with such remains, for extensive traces can also be seen in Nesting, Aithsting, Delting and Northmavine (particularly around Mavis Grind) and also in the more remote parts of Yell and Whalsay. Even the more remote islands, such as Fair Isle, Out Skerries and Foula, were clearly well-settled and have many remains which seem to belong to this period.

Although these ancient archaeological landscapes are complex, they can be broken down into elements: houses and other structures which once had roofs,

clearance cairns, field dykes and major boundary dykes. In addition there are many larger cairns, some with burial chambers, which are a sign of more than economic activity. Finally, there is a vast array of hidden evidence, usually revealed only upon excavation, for crops, livestock, tools and other artefacts.

Around 160 houses have so far been identified in the style which was once known as "Neolithic – Bronze Age", but are now usually simply called "prehistoric", because we know this house type continued well into the Iron Age. Sometimes, for brevity and in tribute to their first investigator, the term "Calder" houses is used. A typical house ruin is a low oval bank of rubble with a hollow centre and with the inner and outer face of the wall formed of large boulders. The central hollow may show traces of alcoves around each side, with the entrance marked by a depression running in from one end. The inner ends of the entrance, and the projections between alcoves, may be formed by large upright stones ("orthostats" in archaeological jargon). Overall house dimensions vary considerably, but something in the order of 10m by 7m externally is normal. Often the foundations of such houses occur in little clusters of three or four, associated with field walls which straggle off across the surrounding landscape.

Excavations at Ness of Gruting, Gruting School, Stanydale, Sumburgh and Scord of Brouster have given us a good idea of the construction of these houses. Walls are thick, faced with heavy stones and cored with smaller rubble and earth, a technique used until very

A large prehistoric house above The Loch That Ebbs and Flows, Papa Stour, showing the large upright slabs which helped support the roof and divide the interior.

recently all over the Highlands and Islands. The interior had two distinct levels. A lower central area generally held a large hearth, upon which peat was burned. Small, stone-lined drains ran from this area under the entrance passage and away downslope. The alcoves around the inside face of the house wall were set higher than the central area, sometimes with raised sills and paved floors. These are generally interpreted as bed or storage recesses. In the course of excavation and field survey a second, less frequent, type of house plan has been noted. Also oval, this lacks the internal alcoves and instead has one or two small oval chambers within the wall thickness. Both plans may be accompanied by a curving wall outside the entrance, combining the function of porch and windbreak – essential in Shetland.

Because only foundations survive, reconstruction of the original form of these houses must be tentative. Evidence of holes for supporting posts and parallels with similar structures of later date would

suggest that the low walls may have been heightened a little with turf, and the whole roofed with thatch, usually heather over sod, carried on a framework of relatively small timbers. The large upright stones in the interior of many houses would have acted as footings for roofing members, serving to reduce the length of load-bearing timbers needed to create the roof structure. This might hint at a shortage of sizeable timber from an early date.

Inside, these houses would have been low, dark and smoky – but no more so than quite recent blackhouses of the north and west. As many daily tasks as possible would have taken place outside, with the inhabitants perhaps sitting on the doorstep in rainy weather, to chip away at making stone implements or to knead clay for pottery-making.

Although these houses often occur alone, in many places they form little clusters of up to six. It is not known if these were true villages, with all the houses in use at once, or if they are simply the ruins of a succession of isolated homes for succeeding generations of one family, each replacing an older house when it became too small or too hard to repair and was relegated to use as a storehouse or barn, as happened on Shetland crofts until much more recent times. At Scord of Brouster, the cluster of houses there seemed to represent the latter situation, but it would be rash to conclude that there were no villages at this time. If these existed, they would presumably have been on the richest land, and therefore most likely to have been subsequently removed.

Shetland's prehistoric farming settlements are usually found near to fresh water but generally stand some distance from the sea, characteristically located behind the best land as seen from the sea. This makes economic sense, as it would be wasteful to build a house on the best cropland. The finest surviving examples are in higher and more remote locations than more recent settlements, consistent with the evidence of a better climate in the Neolithic period. There were undoubtedly many prehistoric farms on land near to the sea, but being on lower and more fertile ground these will have been destroyed or built over in later centuries. This still happens: only a few years ago a prehistoric house was quarried away unnoticed while land was being levelled for a new house not far north of Lerwick, and only identified (too late) from characteristic pottery sherds found in the dumped rubble.

Around these farmhouses and sometimes spreading out for a considerable distance, are found numerous mounds of medium-sized stones. These are usually part-buried in peat and may show only a small patch of stone at the surface, yet on excavation may be found to cover several square metres and reach heights of up to a metre. These mounds represent the results of many generations of field clearance. They are characteristically sorted, with larger stones towards the base and smaller stones higher up. This represents the process of field and soil creation: the largest boulders are hauled aside to make the outlines of fields or to be used in houses. Then the soil is broken up, with the largest stones being thrown onto the walls or onto heaps within the field. As time goes by, smaller and smaller stones are removed, eventually creating a smooth tilth which can easily be ploughed or turned with a mattock or spade.

These clearance cairns today often stand in very poor soil, posing the question of what has happened since the Neolithic period to reduce soil fertility so drastically. The answer seems to be a compound one. Undoubtedly, Shetland's pre-agricultural soils, at least on the lower ground, were deeper and richer, of the type referred to as "brown forest soils". We know this because pockets of such soils sometimes survive, sealed beneath the walls of prehistoric fields and houses. Over the years, weathering alone tends to reduce soil fertility, especially once tree cover is no longer present. The climatic deterioration which began in Neolithic times and continued for two thousand years would have accentuated this, literally washing the goodness from the soil. Also, as the climate became cooler, soil micro-organisms became less efficient at incorporating new organic material into the soil structure.

These natural processes were almost certainly compounded by farming activities. The repeated removal of stones to facilitate cultivation, especially the loss of smaller material which helps to form the structure of the soil and moderates drainage, would have increased the likelihood of waterlogging as the climate became more moist, accelerating the loss of soil nutrients and in extreme cases leading to soil simply washing away. There is evidence from studies of prehistoric soils at Old Scatness and on Papa Stour that manuring and the addition of domestic organic refuse such as peat ash was practised by the end of the Bronze Age, but it is not known how early such practices began. They may have been an invention of necessity for a population who had seen their most precious asset, the soil, literally wasting away from generation to generation. Certainly they came too late to halt the deterioration of soils on the upper hillsides, where settlements were progressively abandoned and the land became covered in peat.

Running among the scattered clearance cairns are stretches of tumbled drystone walling which appear to split the land into small fields of irregular plan. These walls often link clearance cairns together so as to leave the maximum plantable area clear. Excavation of stretches of walling at Scord of Brouster showed that, like the cairns, these walls are often much more substantial than appears on the surface. Sometimes walls link pre-existing cairns, but sometimes it is the walls which are earlier and had small cairns added to them. This suggests that the processes of creating the walls and clearing the soil for cultivation overlapped, with the walls in some cases dividing patches of land worked by different families and in some cases simply acting as elongated clearance heaps.

Even allowing for their tumbled condition, it is hard to envisage these walls as stock-proof barriers, especially for Shetland sheep, which can clear considerable heights when alarmed. But it may be that the surviving stones, which often appear as lines of what one archaeologist has called "perched blocks", are the surviving parts of boundaries constructed partly of stone and partly of turf, as may still sometimes be seen today, for example in parts of Unst – what are locally called "feelie dykes" (from *feal*, meaning turf). So it is possible that these unimpressive-looking walls may in fact have reached respectable heights. This, like so many other problems in Shetland archaeology, awaits more thorough investigation.

In a rather different category are the ruined but still very substantial dykes which run more or less continuously across country, sometimes for kilometres on end. These are much more massive and often run nearly straight, apparently aligned on hilltops or burial cairns. They seem to disregard the quality of the land for agriculture, often crossing stretches of moor which have never been cultivated, even in the relatively balmy climatic days of the earliest faming settlement. The stones in these dykes may be very large indeed, and because of their solid nature and the large amount of available stone in them, some of these ancient walls continue to function, in modified form, as boundaries between scattalds (township grazing lands). Whether this represents continuity of boundaries over thousands of years or simply later re-use is debatable and would be hard to test archaeologically with current methods.

Good examples of such massive dykes can be seen to the north of the road to Walls just west of Bridge of Walls, and south of the road to Sandness just north-west of Scord of Brouster. The most spectacular of all is the Funzie Girt (1) on Fetlar, which divides the north-eastern portion of that island. A particularly intriguing example runs from above the prehistoric settlement at Brouster north-eastwards into a bog – which clearly grew up after the wall was constructed – emerges on the far side and then runs away uphill into

the distance. Further evidence for the early date of these large walls is seen where they skirt areas of small fields associated with prehistoric houses. Almost invariably, the field dykes appear to run up to these larger walls and stop, sometimes continuing on the far side with a marked displacement, clearly implying the priority of the larger walls.

The major dykes partition the landscape into parcels of 100 to 200 hectares. They may have served to split the available land up between early families of farming settlers. Their location on ridges and hill shoulders makes them look more like estate boundaries than farm walls, although they often link the upper limits of cultivated fields which have long been abandoned, and which must have been cleared early in the history of Shetland agriculture. On the other hand, the massive dykes seem to post-date at least some of the larger burial cairns on hilltops.

Shetland's summit – the chambered cairn on top of Ronas Hill is 450m above sea level – and feels higher. Vegetation and landforms here are sub Arctic in character. The ancient cairn has been much modified in more recent times (44).
Photo: Sue White

Their pattern and location suggest that the early farmers realised, not too long after their arrival, that there would be sufficient demand for land to make the formal division of the islands into territories not only desirable but essential. This implies, at peak, a population of several thousand who were using most of the land in an organised fashion, whether for cultivation or for grazing.

We know that the Neolithic period, despite its "stone age" label, was by no means a period of ignorance, but was in fact characterised by organised agriculture and, as will be seen, an organised religion and great skill in the manufacture of material possessions, both utilitarian and ornamental. Therefore a sophisticated approach to the division and use of land should not be surprising. It may be that the investment of considerable labour in creating boundaries sanctified the possession of land in moral or religious terms, reinforcing physical possession. There is a hint, in all this, of a social structure composed of farming families each working one area of ground, linked (perhaps by kinship) into small regional territories, each coinciding with natural land units: half an island or the drainage basin of a small stream network, for example.

Larger cairns, which often stand on hilltops, were constructed as burial places for the dead, reminding us that some of the earliest evidence for Neolithic Shetland is from a burial place, the Sumburgh cist. The Sumburgh burial site is unusual for two reasons. First, it is a simple stone box or coffin set into the ground, without an overlying cairn: this is a

A typical hill shoulder location for a cairn at Vatnabrenda, near West Burrafirth.

burial practice which, throughout Scotland, is usually associated with the succeeding Bronze Age. Second, unusually for Shetland, it contained surviving human remains. Soils in Shetland are generally acid, which means that survival of bone in any burial site is rare, and only the stone structures of the cairns survive, so much of what we can say about their contents is based on inference from elsewhere, especially Orkney.

The typical Neolithic burial place is a stone cairn containing a small slab-roofed chamber, accessed by a narrow entrance passage. Into the chamber were placed the remains of the dead, often over many generations. Burial cairns seem to start being built quite early in the history of the Neolithic, and it may be that building one signified the permanent annexation of an area of land for settlement. Later on, the chambered cairns, with their provision for repeated access to the burial chamber, came to be superseded by cairns of similar size, but which now sealed one or more stone-built burial cists, each of which

Crescentic facades are typical of Shetland's chambered cairns, which tend to be small compared with other regions – South Houllan, near Clousta.

beginning. There may be many more unmarked cist burials to be found – they are obviously less easy to locate than burials under large cairns, and are only found by chance.

The many chambered cairns which occupy such splendidly prominent positions on hilltops are often rather disappointing on closer inspection. Of the long cairns which are so numerous in Orkney, only two, both rather unconvincing, have been identified. The more common form of chambered cairn is a Shetland speciality: the so-called "heel-shaped" cairn. These are circular or squarish on plan, with a distinctive concave façade along one side. From the centre of the façade, which is often more carefully built than the rest of the cairn's perimeter, the narrow entrance passage leads back into the burial chamber. This chamber is commonly sub-rectangular, with one or more small alcoves opening off the main area.

seems to represent a single burial episode. Finally, cairns were abandoned completely in favour of simple small cists with inhumation or cremation burials which were often accompanied by pottery vessels. Although cist-burials, with or without cairns, are usually thought of as Bronze Age in date, the Sumburgh site reminds us that cist-burial was practised from the

The burial chambers of Neolithic cairns tend to be very small compared with the size of the cairn itself, as here at Islesburgh, near Mavis Grind (48).

The roof of the chamber is usually formed by corbelling (building stones gradually inwards) with alcoves and passage roofed with large flat lintel slabs, sometimes of great size and weight.

Heel-shaped cairns vary greatly in size, from massive piles such as Punds Water (47), Vementry (53) and Ronas Hill (44) to miniature versions such as Pettigarth's Field (39). In diameter, they vary from 20 metres to under 4 metres. Some of the larger cairns seem to have been built in two stages, with the burial chamber in an original round cairn which was then augmented to create a massive outer kerb and the distinctive façade. Unlike many chambered cairns in more southerly parts, these façades seem to have been added while the cairns were in use for burial, not as embellishments after they were sealed up and abandoned.

Concave façades have also been noted on a number of house sites, notably at the houses excavated at Sumburgh during airport extensions in the 1970s. This might suggest that cairns were copying domestic plans to provide "houses of the dead" – or, conversely, that houses copied cairns in plan, to form "shrines for the living". At Sumburgh, the façades were clearly added to existing houses, paralleling the suggested two-phase sequence of elaboration of the cairns.

Both cairn-burial and cist-burial reflect a measure of special treatment on death only for certain individuals, since it seems unlikely that there were enough of these elaborate burial places for everyone who died to be given a resting place in one. This observation would apply especially to cists below cairns, each of which could be used only once. The chambered cairns could be used repeatedly, by tidying away the remains of older burials to make way for fresh ones. Evidence from elsewhere suggests that older remains may have been bagged and carefully "filed" in side alcoves, or even that the dead were exposed outside the cairns for some time, until they had decayed sufficiently to be mere skeletons, before being interred.

But the general impression is that there was not a special burial place under a cairn for everyone. What happened to the majority? Presumably they were interred without any special provision of a stone coffin or marker cairn, but they might equally have been cremated, or buried at sea. Only the minority, just a few individuals in each generation, were buried with special rites in a carefully-built cairn overlooking the farmland and the sea.

How one "qualified" for special burial is one of the most hotly-debated archaeological questions. It might have been membership of a family who provided leaders or priests, or it might have been something much more tenuous – perhaps a propitious time of birth or a particular combination of physical features. Work outside Shetland on assemblages of bone fragments from chambered cairns shows that those buried within them may contain both sexes and the complete age range, from infants to the elderly (which in Neolithic times may have meant one's late 30s). As yet no convincing anatomical family traits have been identified in the

The unique late Neolithic structure at Stanydale – temple, feasting place or community hall. It is located out of sight of the sea, and it appears to have been fully roofed, never an easy achievement in Shetland. Its impressive modern appearance owes much to rebuilding after excavation in the mid 20th century (18).

individuals within any one tomb, although current advances with DNA analysis may provide a new way of addressing this question.

Reinforcing this idea of some sort of social elite, mention must be made of two sites which were identified as "prehistoric temples" in the 1940s. This attribution was made by Charles Calder in the days when every innovation in British prehistory was seen as coming from the Mediterranean, and his suggestion was based on the similarity of plan between his Shetland excavation and published plans for ritual sites in Malta such as Hal Tarxien and Mnaidra. Whether Calder had ever visited Malta is not certain: one suspects not, for close acquaintance with both Shetland and Malta sites would have emphasised the many differences

which are far stronger than the similarities of ground plan.

Now that more prehistoric houses have been excavated and planned, the so-called temple at Yoxie in Whalsay (3) can be seen to be a fairly ordinary house, with its "forecourt" simply a windbreak at the door. But the "temple" at Stanydale is a very different case. Now partially restored and with its outer walls heightened to discourage access by sheep, the Stanydale site has a fairly normal house-plan, with the usual alcoves around the inside of the walls and a fine concave façade flanking the entrance. Its remarkable feature is its great size: it is about twice as large as any other excavated house, measuring no less than 13 metres by 6 metres internally. Most other Shetland prehistoric houses could comfortably be dropped inside the

Stanydale structure, with room to spare.

Excavation finds included fragments of large pottery vessels of late Neolithic type, a few typical but not outstanding stone artefacts and some fragments of Bronze Age pottery. Notably, there were hardly any of the ubiquitous roughly-made stone agricultural implements, mattocks and plough points, which usually occur in great abundance on contemporary house sites. Also, there was distinct evidence that this structure was roofed, with the roof supported on two substantial posts of spruce. Since spruce did not grow in Britain, this must be driftwood, presumably brought across by the North Atlantic Drift from North America. Another unusual feature of Stanydale is that it is located in a place where the sea is not visible. This is not easy to achieve in Shetland, where the coast is seldom more than three kilometres away and never more than six. This "inland-ness" echoes the location of other important ritual sites throughout Britain, including many henges and stone circles.

Clearly then, Stanydale was something special, even if it cannot be proven to be a temple in the strictly religious sense. Its scale and the use of massive timbers, which would have been rare in Shetland, together with its location, suggest a communal enterprise. Perhaps it was, indeed, a temple, perhaps simply a village hall. Most puzzling of all, is why there is only one such

structure in all of Shetland. Was it a centre for some activity which served the whole of the islands? Or just a particularly grandiose setting for what, elsewhere, was done in more modest surroundings? Either way, it is exceptional – more exceptional in the Neolithic than even the broch of Mousa is in the Iron Age.

Taking together the evidence of houses, farms and burial places along with that of cairns and dykes, the impression is of a society which appreciated an orderly and settled life. These farmers apparently agreed large-scale land divisions. They respected at least some of their dead and built them special resting places. These traits imply that their desire was to live out their lives in whatever place they found themselves. The chambered tombs and the Stanydale building argue for a society which was sufficiently well organised to arrange large building projects, and such projects would presumably have required supervision and direction. Some form of ruling or directing class seems a likely feature of such a society, perhaps in the form of priests or tradition-bearers rather than warlords or nobles. That there was such a class, archaeology can only infer. It cannot address questions such as how membership of such an elite was acquired, or what privileges and duties accompanied such status. As always, our abilities end just where the really interesting questions begin.

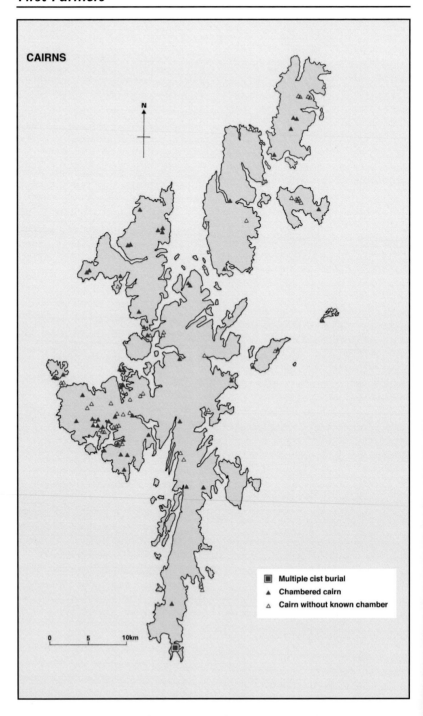

CAIRNS

N

■ Multiple cist burial
▲ Chambered cairn
△ Cairn without known chamber

0   5   10km

Pots and Bones and Stones: Everyday Technology

ALTHOUGH the ruins of early constructions are the most obvious evidence of life in prehistoric Shetland, much of our detailed knowledge about this period has been gained from the study of tools, utensils and ornaments, items which archaeologists refer to as "artefacts", meaning objects fashioned by man. Arguably, a building is an artefact too, but the convention is to divide architecture from artefacts. There are many features of Shetland's early architecture which are hard to parallel elsewhere, which makes it hard to devise chronologies for different building types, but with one notable exception all the main types of artefact found in Shetland are found elsewhere in northern Britain. This allows comparison and relative dating between different regions — provided of course the artefacts in question are from a known context. Objects which are chance finds and cannot be related to a specific horizon of a named site are referred to disparagingly as "stray finds" – although even they can have some value, especially when collected over a large area.

Before the days of radiocarbon dating, which gives (almost) absolute ages based upon changes in the proportions of isotopes in the carbon of once-living materials, like bone and wood, comparison of artefacts provided relative dates, both for the artefacts and for the sites from which they came. The well-known Three Ages system, originally devised in Denmark – Stone Age, Bronze Age, Iron Age – remains in popular use. Archaeologists have increasingly sub-divided these basic periods. The Stone Age for example has been divided into the Old, Middle and New Stone Age, now usually Palaeolithic, Mesolithic and Neolithic, themselves usually subdivided again and again, to produce terms such as "the Late Middle Palaeolithic".

As study has advanced, these periods have been redefined, and now relate mainly to non-artefactual factors: the Neolithic, for example, is generally recognised as a period in which sedentary agricultural life becomes the norm. The fact that it was originally defined by reference to the widespread appearance of polished stone axes is not particularly important. It is possible nowadays, as indeed Shetland perfectly well illustrates, to possess a respectable local Bronze Age even if hardly any bronze artefacts have been found, provided that other characteristics of the period are present: distinctive pottery types, single burials in cists, a gradual move to cremation, and so on.

But artefactual studies remain important. They tell us a great deal about how people lived their daily lives, and also provide evidence for local and long-distance trade. In a few cases we have been lucky enough to find places where artefacts were made, allowing us to cross-check our theories about how early industries operated. In addition, many prehistoric technologies are still in use somewhere around the world, in "primitive" societies. Much can be gained by looking at these "ethnographic parallels", even though they are seldom quite as parallel as we might wish.

Most raw materials available everywhere in early Britain were also available to early Shetlanders. There was abundant clay for pottery, stone of many types, wood occurred in reasonable quantities and bone and horn, too, would have been abundant in the semi-pastoral economy which Shetland has practised from the earliest days. Each type of stone would have characteristics which suited it for a different purpose – some to be polished, some to be split, some to be chipped. Likewise every different bone of every different animal – and often of different ages of each animal – had a particular use, from the finest of fishbone needles to the largest of cattle shoulder-blade shovels.

Added to these relatively durable materials, artefacts of which often survive, would have been a huge array of more perishable materials, long-since rotted away. Leather and sinew, or heather and straw, for example. Recent northern societies, such as the Inuit or the Sámi, show great knowledge and sophistication in the use of animal hide and bird skins, each serving a different purpose according to its durability, flexibility, softness and waterproof qualities. And let anyone who doubts the importance of heather and straw visit the Shetland Museum to see the range of items made from them well into modern times. Shetland being Shetland, we can assume that wool quickly became an important product, and provided most of the everyday clothing of the inhabitants – even though, archaeologically, we cannot demonstrate weaving before the Iron Age. Interestingly, there seems to be no consensus at all upon when and where knitting was invented.

Because of the poor conditions for preservation in Shetland's acidic soils, usually it is only pottery and stone which survive, with sometimes a little bone and, if the site is waterlogged, wood. These are the artefacts recovered from excavations and as chance finds. It is important to remember that all of the artefacts we study have had to survive the intervening millennia and must have been sufficiently manmade to have been noticed and retrieved for study. This means we are looking at a portion, perhaps quite a small portion, of the equipment of the well-provided Neolithic Shetlander. We cannot study what has not been preserved, or what has been preserved but not noticed.

It is noticeable that many of the artefacts we find have been made with more care than was strictly necessary from a utilitarian viewpoint, and may well have been treasured possessions. Being carefully made, they are easier to spot in the ground. Doubtless there were disposable tools in the Neolithic as there are today – pebbles split to provide a sharp edge to gut a fish, and then discarded, or bones splintered to bore holes in leather or wood. Identifying these is not always easy, even on properly conducted excavations, as it may require microscopic examination of each and every fragment.

Pottery studies are very important to prehistoric archaeology, because changing vessel styles can help to assign sites to different periods, and can also suggest which sites were in use at the same time. Although some combinations of vessel shape and decoration are long-lived, they tend not to be re-invented: once out of date, pottery styles seem to stay out of date.

All of Shetland's prehistoric pottery is hand-made, for the potter's wheel does not seem to have been introduced here until relatively recently. Early pottery was made by building up coils of clay onto a flat base, then smoothing the pot prior to decorating the outer surface with incised lines or applied bands of clay ("cordons" in archaeological parlance). Finally, the pot would be fired in a small kiln.

Prehistoric pottery tends to be gritty and coarse. Broken shreds may resemble fine-grained sandstone and easily pass unnoticed by the untrained eye. Vessels vary in size and form, including a range of bowls and bucket-shapes. Most pots were used for storage of food and water. Some were strong enough to be used for cooking, although they were easily broken by careless handling or extremes of temperature, especially sudden cooling. Blackened fragments of clay cooking pot are a common find on excavations, and the charred residues can tell us about contemporary diet: not surprisingly, vegetable-based porridges and gruels seem to be common, with or without milk. Not all cooking required pots, of course: meat and fish could be roasted on flat stones, or grilled on a rotating spit.

Although some of the decorative motifs on Shetland Neolithic pots suggest links with Orkney, there are distinct differences, and some widespread types do not occur. There do not seem to have been any special vessels made to accompany burials into cairns or cists. Later on, marking the transition to the Bronze Age, a few of the ubiquitous "beaker" style pots occur, and these do seem to have been luxury items, perhaps made specially for funeral rites. But in Shetland beakers are few in number and do not seem to be of local manufacture.

Clay was not the only material used to make durable containers. A Shetland speciality was the carving of vessels out of steatite, a fibrous rock which can be shaped with stone tools. (The popular name for steatite is soapstone, because of its greasy feel and shiny surface.) This rock occurs in a number of places around Shetland, notably at Catpund in Cunningsburgh (129). It was used to produce carved vessels and ornaments. Small chips of steatite were also used as a filler in clays for pottery-making. These characteristics were attractive to potters, for clay containing steatite can be polished to a high gloss. It may be that much of the steatite filler used in clay potting began life as carved vessels and was re-cycled after these were broken.

By the end of the Neolithic, steatite vessels and pottery containing steatite was to be found in farmhouse kitchens many miles from the nearest outcrop of the rock, raising the tantalising question of whether outcrops were "owned" and vessels traded, or whether anybody could just go to the rock-source and quarry it. We can be sure that Neolithic Shetlanders had an excellent knowledge of all the natural resources of their islands, but we do not have much evidence about how more restricted resources such as steatite were controlled and managed. On the grounds that human nature does not change too

Pots and Bones and Stones: Everyday Technology

rapidly, it seems fair to assume that those who lived in an area with something that their neighbours coveted would have taken some advantage, although it might at first have been a social advantage rather than an economic one.

We can also reasonably assume that all craft activities were accompanied with a degree of appropriate ritual, and that skilled exponents of their crafts were recognised and their products valued over less stylish items. It is perfectly possible that there were signature styles belonging to particular potters, whose output was destined to sit on the dresser rather than hide in the darkness of the larder. While speculating, it may be worth wondering if in fact *all* fired clay and stone vessels were special, and restricted to cooking and other specific purposes: one thinks of the modern distinction between the best china for visitors and cheaper plastic or metal kitchenware – except instead of plastic and metal the Neolithic kitchen might have had containers and plates of wood, bark, woven twigs and even animal skin. Such vessels would have been lighter and less fragile, more suited to transporting goods for trade or simply for accompanying people as they moved about the landscape on their daily business.

While pottery can be hard enough to identify when broken, and bone, wood and other organic materials are elusive on most sites, worked stone can be very easy to identify – it just "does not look natural". Thus it is that the majority of stray finds from this period are stone artefacts.

The earliest stone tools found in Shetland are very basic in concept.

At Jarlshof (25) split pebbles were used as knives in the earliest phases of the occupation of the site, and later came to be accompanied by a wide range of crude but effective tools chipped out of flat slabs of local slatey sandstone: saws, knives, choppers and chisels may all be recognised. This "slate" was easy to work, but the tools rapidly lost their edge, and can only have been used a few times before becoming broken or blunted. Such tools were effectively disposable, and many sites with suitable rocks nearby had their own rough and ready toolkit of obviously worked lumps of stone to which it is often hard to ascribe a definite category or purpose. Archaeologists of an earlier generation took to calling such things "rude stone implements" – "rude" meaning merely roughly-finished, to the disappointment of young archaeologists of less refined generations!

Tougher-grained sandstones were in demand for making agricultural implements, of which two forms are very common. One is what appears to be the blade of a mattock, a chopping tool used for breaking up and turning the soil. These were made by chipping down a flat lump of sandstone, about 30 by 15 centimetres and 4-6 centimetres thick. Mattock blades are usually rough-surfaced except for their working ends, which are distinctively smooth or even polished due to wear. Presumably these blades were mounted in a handle or haft. The second form, plough-tips, or "ard-points", are also frequent finds. These are elongated bars of sandstone with a circular cross-section, tapered towards one end and showing signs of wear around the pointed end. This wear arises from their function as the cutting point of a primitive wooden stilt-plough, or "ard". Examples of wooden ards have been found in Shetland bogs, and a good example is in the Shetland Museum, so we know what they looked like. Ards would have been pulled by cattle or horses, which had by now reached Shetland, or perhaps even, one suspects reluctantly, by humans.

It is always good when archaeology proves something beyond doubt, and in the mid 1980s, during excavations at Kebister, beside Dales Voe, evidence for the use of such implements was found. Not only was there the typical scratching of the sub-soil caused by ard-ploughing, but in some cases there were ard-points actually embedded at the end of furrows, where they had broken off on impact with earth-fast stones. It is generally thought that ards were used to break up tough surfaces, on land which had not been ploughed before, or had lain fallow for many years, and then mattocks were used to turn the soil over to create a seed-bed. So far, we have not found a mattock-blade embedded in an ancient field, so we cannot be quite so positive about how they were used.

Both mattocks and ard-points occur in huge numbers – some excavations of prehistoric house sites have produced literally tons of them. This indicates they were frequently broken and were a readily-made and discarded commodity. Even the later introduction of iron did not supersede them completely, and there is at least one example of an ard point in a Shetland farming history collection which may have been in use until the early 19th century AD.

There is one other widespread, if not exactly common, sandstone "tool" which continues to puzzle archaeologists. This is the "Shetland club". A number of these odd artefacts have been found during ploughing. They are carefully made, smooth-surfaced sandstone bars with an oval cross-section, and may be anything up to 80 centimetres long. Some have what look likes a narrow handle at one end, and they are often decorated with simple incised lines. Although looking rather like clumsy cricket-bats, these "clubs" would have been awkward to hold and very ineffective as weapons. Their purpose remains unknown and since none has come from an excavated context there is doubt about their exact date, although they "look prehistoric". Once again, the Shetland Museum has some fine examples.

Sandstone served well enough for tools which had to be tough but did not need to be very sharp, but it was not suitable for every purpose. In particular, it could not provide razor-sharp cutting edges or long-lasting scrapers for preparing hide, or arrow-heads. Nor could heavy woodworking tools be made of sandstone. In most parts of Europe, small sharp tools were made from flint, a form of quartz which resembles an impure glass. In the hands of an expert flint can be flaked to create a wide variety of shapes with extremely sharp edges. Unfortunately for prehistoric Shetland, flint does not outcrop in the islands. Although it does occur

Neolithic arrowheads made of several types of stone.
Photo: Shetland Museum

as small beach pebbles, these are usually flawed and unsuitable for delicate shaping. The nearest reliable flint sources are in Aberdeenshire, although there is some acceptably high quality beach flint along the shores of Sanday and North Ronaldsay in Orkney.

In the absence of flint, Shetlanders experimented with flaking a variety of rocks. The favourite, and closest in character to flint, was quartz. This can produce sharp edges, but is much harder to work, as it does not have a predictable fracture pattern. Quartz tools are found, in the form of arrow-heads and small knives and scrapers, but these lack the elegance of their flint counterparts. They are also harder to spot as stray finds, since small chips and flakes of quartz occur naturally in most Shetland soils. There are a few arrow-heads of flint in Shetland. These may have been made locally from a rare

unflawed beach pebble or from an imported block of flint, or they may have been brought to Shetland ready-made.

In contrast, heavier tools such as axes, which had to retain a reasonably, but not razor-sharp, edge, were usually made by polishing close-grained igneous rock, and here Shetland is well-provided, especially in the North Mainland around Ronas Hill, where there are many small outcrops of fine-grained igneous rocks such as felsite within the red granite which forms Shetland's highest hill. Polished stone tools are much more common stray finds than quartz or flint implements: they are larger and their smooth surfaces gleam when wet, attracting the passing eye.

The most characteristic tool-type of the Neolithic is the polished stone axe. Such axes were made by flaking out a rough shape from a block of close-grained rock, and then rubbing it down against another block of stone to produce a smooth surface. Sometimes the finish is so polished that it must have been created by using fine sand or some other abrasive medium in the final stages. Shaped like an elongated and flattened pear, stone axes vary from as little as ten centimetres in length up to over 40, although 25 centimetres is the norm. They have a broad flat end with a strong sharp edge, ground down from both sides, and a narrower, unsharpened end, which was fitted into a wooden haft.

Stone axes are often found in a well-used condition, with evidence for re-sharpening and chips to the cutting edge. Tests have shown that these axes are quite capable of cutting down trees, but there is also evidence that they were valued in their own right. There are miniature axes which occur from time to time, looking like toys or amulets, and the very high polish on some axes suggests they were made more as things of beauty than as utilitarian objects.

A much rarer stone artefact-type, associated with the end of the Neolithic period, is the mace-head. These again are polished from close-grained rock. They are usually short tapered cylinders with blunt ends, and have a cylindrical hafting hole bored through their mid-point. When complete, they would have looked like nothing so much as the gavel of a committee chairman, but the archaeological convention is to regard them as ornamental weapons. Mace-heads are very distinctive and occur throughout Britain.

But pride of place in the polished stone tool catalogue must go to Shetland's unique artefact-type, the "Shetland knife". These beautiful but puzzling artefacts are thin oblongs of polished rock, with rounded corners, and usually measure from 15 to 20 centimetres long. They were made by flaking out a very thin block and then grinding this from both sides to produce a plate of rock as little as four millimetres thick. A sharp edge was created all around the perimeter of this plate, but one side was then blunted before use – presumably to aid hafting, or at least to allow it to be safely held in the hand. Like the stone axes, the knives were capable of use, for damaged and re-sharpened examples occur, but the majority have been found in almost new condition.

Earlier editions of this guide referred to a solitary example of a Shetland knife from Clydesdale, but when this artefact was finally located and examined, it was clear that the old label's Victorian handwriting had been misread: rather than "Lanark" it clearly said "Lerwick": a reminder of the need always to look at the

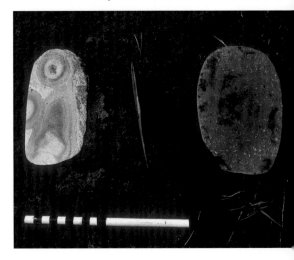

Stone knives: a late Neolithic speciality of Shetland (the photographic scale is 30cm long overall). Part of the hoard of 19 found by the author in the late 1970s, in eroding peat near the summit of Stourabrough Hill, West Mainland.

original, and not accept second-hand evidence! That example disposed of, these beautiful and skilfully-made artefacts do, indeed, seem to be unique to Shetland. This is a real puzzle, for not only do these knives not occur anywhere else – they are unknown in Orkney or the Scottish Mainland – but there are no artefacts in neighbouring areas which look even remotely like them.

This makes their function hard to explain. Looking for parallels among later tools, the closest seem to be in leatherworking, where metal knives of similar profile were used to shave off very fine layers of hide, especially in bookbinding. It has often been suggested that Shetland's stone knives might be for cutting up stranded whales, or preparing sealskins. But of course whales and seals occur in other parts of the Atlantic seaboard, without similar knives being found. It may be that these knives represent some practice which was widespread but for some reason attained "cult status" only in Shetland – and here something to do with marine life seems a likely guess. Having attained cult status, the tools of the trade, which were normally quite undistinguished, began to be made in beautiful, ornamental versions, to be owned and treasured by experts of whatever skill they represented. A far-fetched parallel would be with Masonic regalia, which reproduce in precious materials the emblematic tools of the mason's trade.

Despite having to guess about their exact function, we can say something about the status of polished stone artefacts in society, and even more about their manufacture and distribution.

Shetland knives, and sometimes axes as well, are often found in small groups during peat-cutting, often high on hillsides. The fact that the artefacts in such hoards are sometimes carefully arranged argues against them being accidentally lost – perhaps a bag-load dropped from a pack-horse – and in favour of them being deliberately buried. One group was spread out in a circle, while another group of 19 stone knives was arranged like books on a shelf, complete with two sandstone blocks to form "bookends". It may be that burying knives and axes in peat for a period was part of the manufacturing process, part functional, part ritual – a little like maturing cheese or whisky. But it seems more probable that these are offerings to some deity or power. The practice of burying valuable objects in wet places is known throughout North West Europe in the Bronze Age and Iron Age, but is less well-attested from the Neolithic. It is tempting to see these hoards, buried on hilltops and other areas where peat was actively growing, as treasures given up to the Gods in the hope of reversing climatic deterioration, but in fact sacrifices of valuables simply seem to be a part of standard religious practice at this period.

By a fortunate chance, many Shetland polished stone artefacts are made of rare rock. This is a speckled or banded felsite, an intrusive igneous rock, which occurs on the slopes of Ronas Hill – Shetland's highest point. Unlike many of the rocks used for Neolithic axes, this rock is so distinctive it does not usually require microscopic examination to identify it. So objects

made of it can readily be identified wherever they are found. Axes and at least one mace-head of this distinctive felsite are known from outside Shetland, while the knives are only found locally.

Interestingly, axes and mace-heads of non-Shetland stone are known from within Shetland, including an axe from near Sullom which is from the well-known axe factories on the slopes of Great Langdale in the English Lake District. But no knives made of non-local rock are known. This suggests that axes and mace-heads were being exchanged or traded, sometimes over quite long distances (although perhaps passed from hand to hand, rather than in single-long distance movements). They were of value in themselves, and may even have formed a means of exchange, like an early currency. But knives seem to have been valued only locally, and neither left nor came into the islands.

Some decades ago, a major site for axe and knife production was identified at the Beorgs of Uyea on the desolate moorland north of Ronas Hill, where a shelter made of large granite blocks (itself perhaps relatively recent) roofs a long cutting alongside one of the best outcrops of the characteristic felsite. This cutting had been made by quarrying blocks off the outcrop, and all around were scattered fragments of flaked rock, including blanks for axes and knives which had broken in production, or been rejected as sub-standard. The dark felsite shows up clearly against the surrounding reddish granite. Since that discovery, other smaller working areas have been found around the flanks of the hill.

Beorgs of Uyea near North Roe, on the northern slopes of Ronas Hill. The distinctive dark outcrop was the principal quarry for stone axes and knives (5).

Pots and Bones and Stones: Everyday Technology

The felsite quarry sites are high above any likely settlement and very exposed, so it seems that the axes and knives were blocked out on site, but taken away for polishing. Evidence for this may be found in the absence of part-polished fragments around the outcrop, and also in a few axe and knife rough-outs found in other parts of Shetland, far from the source. As with steatite, there is no evidence to tell us if anyone had free access to this valuable resource, or if it was controlled by one particular group.

If Shetland is fortunate in having a major Neolithic tool production site, it is unfortunate in that we have very few reliable dates for when these tools were in use. The large majority are stray finds, and they are rare on excavations, although small fragments of polished stone knives have been found in broch excavations, raising the intriguing concept of Iron Age antiquarianism. We know that elsewhere in Scotland, broch-dwellers collected exotic objects – Roman and continental European items appear on several sites – so perhaps we should not be too surprised to find attractive looking older objects of local origin, too. This collecting may go back earlier: from Stanydale came a much re-sharpened miniature stone axe, which from its excavation context appears to have been lost in the later Bronze Age. Only one dig has produced axes and knives together, but this, at Modesty in West Mainland, took place long before the days of radiocarbon dating, and we know little of the circumstances, except that the site appeared to contain ash and late Neolithic pottery.

It is possible that most of Shetland's stone axes, and also the knives, may have been made during a relatively short-lived period at the end of the Neolithic and the start of the Bronze Age, with the stock of implements thereafter gradually reduced by offerings, breakage and loss. The reason for this suggestion is that some Shetland axes look very like stone copies of early flat bronze axes. The knives, too, are a difficult shape to produce in stone, and have similarities to early copper artefacts, as well as to the earliest bronzes. One possibility is that, around 2000 BC, Shetlanders became aware of the newly-introduced metal technology but lacked bronze or the wherewithal to acquire it, so set about making convincing replicas. Archaeologists use the word "skeuomorph" to describe such an object, made out of the "wrong" material for its form.

Whether or not this speculation has any basis, it does seem that stone-polishing ceased to be practised as a means of making artefacts not long after bronze reached the north of Scotland in quantity. Interestingly, flaking and chipping of flint and quartz, and also of the Shetland felsite, continued. There is a great deal of research still to be done on this topic, for although chipped stone artefact manufacture continued long after metals were introduced, archaeologists have rather tended to ignore it in the Bronze Age and succeeding periods, concentrating instead on the more glamorous topic of metal artefacts.

Before talking about early metallurgy, it is worth a reminder that, just as all containers were not

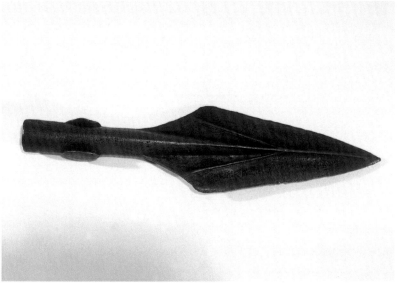

of pottery, so all tools were not of stone. Although bone does not usually survive well in Shetland soils, there are quite a number of bone tools from excavation sites, mainly awls, needles and chisels, plus some nondescript pegs and toggles. Probably bone was widely used. Shoulder-blades of cattle could be used with little modification as mattocks and shovels. Ribs could be sharpened and used as knives for cutting up blubber and meat. One major resource would have been occasional stranded whales, providing meat and oil as well as bone. Whalebone is particularly springy and resilient, and in recent times has seen uses which reflect this, such as umbrella ribs and corset bones. Inuit tents in Greenland and the Canadian Arctic often have whale-rib roof supports, whale vertebrae make useful seats and many a Shetland croft has one in use as a block for chopping firewood.

With all these skills in artefact-making, it would not be surprising to learn that Shetlanders quickly adopted metallurgy when the knowledge of bronze spread north in the centuries after 2000 BC. In fact, this appears not to have been the case. There is hardly any evidence for early bronze-working in Shetland. It is not until the end of this period, around 700 BC or later, that we have evidence for metal-working, at the long-established settlement site of Jarlshof and at nearby Wiltrow.

Nor is there much in the way of imported metalwork, although among the few objects which have been found is a splendid spear-head from Lunnasting. This shortage of bronze objects might be due to Shetland becoming impoverished as a result of climatic deterioration, which was beginning by 2000 BC. This would have limited the possibilities of trade, and Shetland lies far from any bronze sources. (There is copper in Shetland, but no signs of it being worked in early times.) But a far more likely explanation is that bronze was, in fact, imported, but always had a scarcity value. Bronze objects would not have been carelessly lost, and if broken or outmoded they would have been recycled into new items.

From the later Bronze Age, we know of only two smith's workshops, both of which produced ornaments and weapons. Scrap bronze, slag and fragments of moulds and crucibles from both sites indicate that production was taking place on site, either from local ores or, more likely, from imported ingots or scrap metal. The artefacts being produced were of types which were current at the very end of the Bronze Age. It has been suggested that these were the workplaces of immigrant craftsmen, reluctant to learn new skills, who came to Shetland to continue to ply their old-fashioned trade in a backward society, trying to make a quick profit before iron-working reached Shetland. But this seems far-fetched in the extreme. There were perfectly good uses for bronze which did not disappear when iron-working began. Bronze is particularly suited to producing daggers and swords, for example, and it took many centuries after iron was introduced before cold steel replaced quality bronze as the choice for quality weapons.

Probably bronze was a luxury in Shetland throughout the Bronze Age, used mainly for ornaments and decorative purposes. Then, as the Bronze Age gave way to the Iron Age, two linked changes occurred which would stimulate demand for bronze. First, society throughout the north became more unsettled, conflict more common and therefore personal weaponry may have become a harsh necessity rather than an optional adornment. Secondly, there were major changes in building styles, culminating in the brochs. Iron Age buildings were larger and more elaborate, and used more wood. This would have needed heavy tools, such as saws and adzes. Bone handles from just such tools were found in excavations into the early Iron Age levels at Clickimin (21).

Having come far ahead of our time in pursuit of early technology, it is now necessary to return to the end of the Neolithic, around 2000 BC, to see how life changed for Shetland's farming communities as climatic deterioration began to impact upon what nowadays might be called their "lifestyle options".

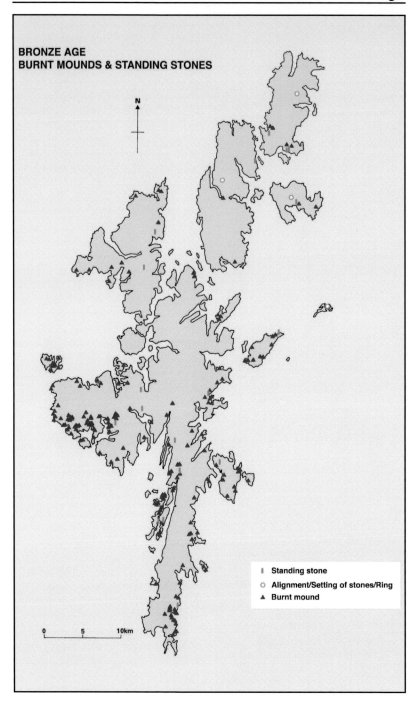

BRONZE AGE
BURNT MOUNDS & STANDING STONES

N

	Standing stone
O	Alignment/Setting of stones/Ring
▲	Burnt mound

0 5 10km

A slow decline? – Shetland's Bronze Age

Shetland's ponies have been here for a long time, certainly since the Bronze Age. They transported heavy loads, and perhaps pulled ploughs, while their long tails and manes provided the strongest natural fibre available to prehistoric man. Mares would have been milked and young animals may have been slaughtered for meat.

ALTHOUGH bronze itself is scarce in the centuries following 2000 BC, many of the changes in society which coincide with the first use of bronze elsewhere do occur in Shetland. So the islands can be said to have a Bronze Age, even though its start is not marked by striking changes. It emerges rather seamlessly from the Neolithic, with new aspects – techniques, buildings and artefacts – gradually appearing, but lifestyles not seeming to change very rapidly. Nonetheless, by the end of the Bronze Age, around 700 BC, life was very different from how it was at the beginning, around 2000 BC.

Throughout this period, climatic change was a major factor in life, and for most of the period the trend was one-way: downhill. Summers grew cooler, winters became colder and stormier, and rainfall rose. The differences were probably not great enough to see in one generation – although doubtless Shetlanders then as now would have reminisced about the balmy summers of their youth – but change was certainly fast enough to be appreciated over the collective memory and tradition of the local population.

What caused these climatic changes, which were felt throughout Europe, is not certain. It may well have been a combination of factors. One contender is a series of particularly violent volcanic eruptions in Iceland. Evidence for these events takes the form of layers of fine volcanic dust interleaved with peat and soil deposits. Nowadays, archaeologists can use such deposits – called *tephra* – as an aid to dating sites, because each layer has a distinctive chemistry and can provide a welcome time horizon across a wide geographical area. They would have been less welcome in the Bronze Age. Large quantities of ash blown into the upper atmosphere could have reflected more of the sun's light and heat, preventing it reaching the surface of the Earth. Added to this global effect, the dust itself, where it fell in sufficient quantities, tended to further acidify already acid soils, reducing their fertility.

Whatever the cause, the result of this climatic downturn was disastrous for Shetland, already near the margins of arable cultivation. Peat, which had formerly occurred

only in limited valleys and loch basins, began to accumulate in ever-deeper quantities all over the higher hill slopes, especially where the soil was exhausted and waterlogged, perhaps through poor husbandry. As time went on, the lower edge of this blanket of peat moved ever downwards, burying much of the Neolithic farmland and ultimately the abandoned dwellings of the farmers themselves. While this has been a blessing for archaeologists, it must have been a disaster for the contemporary inhabitants of Shetland, who would have found themselves gradually forced from the hillsides down to the lower areas around the voes, which would already have been well-peopled.

To add to the inevitable overcrowding of the coastal areas, the slow rise of sea level would have been steadily inundating low-lying land around the shore. This effect was greatest in areas such as Sumburgh, where the gentle offshore slope meant that slight rises in sea level destroyed considerable tracts of flat land.

The cumulative effects of these changes must have been severe. Not only was the arable area reduced, but lower temperatures and more rain would have made crops less reliable, and would have worsened waterlogging, a process which might have been compounded by the trampling of cattle. The farmers made the best they could of this situation, adapting to become less dependent upon crops and more dependent upon their domesticated animals. Probably they were forced to rely more upon marine and coastal resources, although the

The Bronze Age saw the clustering of houses into small villages. In this aerial view of Jarlshof, the Bronze Age village is in the lower centre right, just above the roof of the visitor centre (25).

stormier weather conditions would not have made this easy. There can be little doubt that by the end of the Bronze Age Shetland was supporting more people than it could comfortably accommodate. The results of this were to be felt most keenly in the succeeding Iron Age.

If population density built up so much on the coastal lands, it might seem strange that there is so little archaeological evidence for Bronze Age settlement in these areas, and that so few distinctive artefacts of the period have been found. The explanation probably lies in the fact that, as the climate worsened and living conditions deteriorated, Shetland would simply have been unattractive to newcomers. The settled inhabitants might well have been openly hostile to any new arrivals. Combining this with the lack of any non-essential productivity to provide a surplus to trade for exotic newfangled materials, it is hardly

surprising that there is a general shortage of artefactual evidence for outside contacts in the period 2000-1000 BC.

Most of the houses of this period would have been removed in later years, for they would have been concentrated on what has remained the best farmland ever since. It is in any case almost impossible to distinguish houses of Neolithic date from Bronze Age ones on the superficial appearance of their ruins alone – for example the houses excavated at Sumburgh airport in the mid 1970s were proven to be of Bronze Age date, but this could not have been predicted from their plan alone. Once a type of dwelling suited to the Shetland environment was established, this seems to have stayed in vogue for several thousand years. From the earliest farms of the Neolithic right through into the Iron Age, thick-walled oval houses are the norm. There is some suggestion of

Houses tended to become more circular in the later Bronze Age – an excavated example at Jarlshof (25).

change after 1000 BC, with houses at Jarlshof becoming nearer circular on plan, and their walls rather thinner; which seems odd, bearing in mind the worsening climate, but perhaps people were just too hard-pressed to build as solidly as before.

One distinct change did take place, however. This was in burial practices, perhaps marking a major religious shift. This reflected changes all over Britain, suggesting that Shetland remained connected to wider society, despite the difficult times it was experiencing. Individual rather than collective burial became the usual practice, and over time cremation became more normal than inhumation. The dead began to be buried in small stone boxes, or cists, accompanied by a pottery vessel and often by a few token possessions.

The early Bronze Age is marked, throughout Britain, by the appearance of "beakers" – open-mouthed, vase-like pottery vessels, usually highly decorated with regular patterns of incised lines. These are usually found in stone-built boxes – cists – along with single crouched inhumations, burials where the body is placed on one side with the knees tucked up towards its chin. Shortly after beakers appear, the practice of collective burial within chambered cairns ceases entirely. These changes suggest a radical alteration in religious practices and, by implication, beliefs. Tentatively, one might suggest a move away from a religion with strong ancestor-worship characteristics, where the dead are not regarded as entirely departed but retain a role in ongoing community life, towards

beliefs in which individuals leave the world of the living and proceed to another life elsewhere, one which is not strongly connected with that of those left behind.

Beakers probably contained a drink akin to mead to nourish the deceased in the afterlife, or as an offering to the gods. They are quite rare in Shetland. Sherds of beaker pottery occur at Stanydale, and it may be that they were seen as a valuable exotic rarity, as was Roman pottery in the later Iron Age. By the middle Bronze Age Shetland, with the rest of northern Britain, had

In the Bronze Age, small stone cists replace re-usable burial chambers under cairns, but the preference for elevated locations remains – Pettigarth's Field, Whalsay.

45

developed a range of coarser vessels with beaker-like decoration but much chunkier and less elegant profiles. These are called "food vessels" (for no very good reason, except to contrast with "beakers") and occur with larger and even less elegant pottery "urns", both on domestic sites and with burials. By the middle of the Bronze Age burials seem to be predominantly cremations. Such burials tend to be found by chance, often on low hillocks close to the coastal farmlands where we assume almost everyone was living by this time. But in general, Bronze Age burials in their characteristic stone cists, without cairns over them, are rare finds in Shetland. This prompts speculation about whether or not there were other ways of disposing of the dead – perhaps simply a cremation followed by burial in an unlined pit, which would be almost undetectable in Shetland soil conditions. It is just possible that one or two sites, particularly the Rounds of Tivla (28), may hint at the occurrence in Shetland of the

practice of building enclosed cremation cemeteries – low banks containing areas with pits for cremations, and over the surface of which ashes might simply have been strewn.

One typical monument of the Scottish Bronze Age is almost absent in Shetland. Stones marked with patterns of pecked circular hollows, "cup-marks", are widespread throughout Scotland, usually in early Bronze Age contexts when they can be dated at all. There is only one convincing set of cup-marks in Shetland, at Brough in Whalsay (40), and these are undistinguished by Scottish standards. Since archae-ologists have not yet agreed among various theories about what cup-marked rocks signify, it is impossible to assess the significance of their scarcity in Shetland, while the natural geology of the islands complicates matters still further by providing widespread outcrops of pebbly conglomerate, which often display natural depressions looking temptingly like cup-marks.

The Shetland Bronze Age is typified, as already noted, by many small, gradual changes, rather than by a major revolution in lifestyle. One such change is in the way stone arrow-heads are made. In the Neolithic the usual form is a leaf or lozenge shape, while in the Bronze Age this changes to a triangle with two sharply-angled barbs either side of a protruding tang, which would have been fastened into the shaft. Archaeologists, with typical imagination, call such arrow-heads "barbed and tanged". Such arrow-heads are rare in Shetland, probably because they are very hard to make in any material other than good

Bronze Age "barbed and tanged" arrowheads were not easy to make in quartz rather than flint.
Photo: Shetland Museum

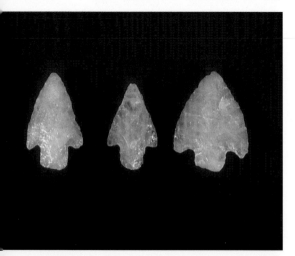

quality flint, and it is likely that the use of quartz, felsite and other flint-substitutes led to the older, leaf-shaped arrow-head continuing as standard equipment throughout the Bronze Age.

Other stone implements also continued from the Neolithic – there is no sign of ard-points or mattocks changing, and it may be that Shetland clubs, mace-heads and possibly Shetland knives were all produced well into the Bronze Age – they certainly occur on sites with Bronze Age as well as Neolithic pottery. Indeed, as hinted at in the previous chapter, it may be that the appearance of the new wonder-material, bronze, rather than depressing stone artefact manu-facturing standards may actually have stimulated stone-workers into competition, thus improving standards and introducing new products.

Another area in which technology

changed during the Bronze Age is indicated by the appearance of large numbers of a new class of monument, the "burnt mound". Always located near to a source of fresh water, a typical burnt mound is kidney-shaped on plan and measures from five to 15m across and up to 2m high, composed of fist-sized fire-cracked and reddened

Food processing changed too: "trough" querns replaced earlier, larger "saddle" querns. This broken example lies beside a prehistoric house on Vementry.

Burnt mounds are the signature monument of the Shetland Bronze Age. This example at Engamoor, near West Burrafirth, shows the hallmarks, location in a boggy hollow, crescent plan and distinctive parched or bare surface.

The "business end" of each burnt mound was a stone trough that held water to be heated. Excavations at Tangwick in Esha Ness revealed this large example. The purpose of the unusual sub-division of the trough is not known.

results in them being very free-draining, so that during dry spells the grass or other vegetation growing upon them becomes parched more quickly than that of their usually boggy surroundings.

It is clear that burnt mounds are essentially about boiling water, by the slow but sure method of adding heated stones to a large trough-full of cold water. Once boiling, the water can be kept simmering by adding a few stones every so often. The technique has been tried and tested and works, in a slow but fuel-efficient way. The mundane explanation is that this was a cooking method employed by a population who want to cook large joints of meat or other bulky foodstuffs, but did not have vessels strong enough and large enough to hang over their fires. Slow-cooking by burnt mound would also be a good way to make use of low-value parts of carcases and left-overs, perhaps mixed with grain: indeed, the Bronze Age may have witnessed the birth of the haggis and similar sausages and puddings.

That burnt mounds are about cooking is supported by the broken fragments of pottery and bone often found mixed with the stones of the mounds. But of course cooking and eating is a very significant activity in social as well as nutritional terms, and the mounds may indicate a period in which the communal preparation and eating of large meals becomes part of accepted social practice: something which might have become ever more significant as times became leaner. This might explain the small "houses" sometimes found buried in the mounds, making these, in effect,

stones and earth. A trough made of stone slabs usually lies within the concave side of the mound, although often it is buried in tumbled stone from the mound. Excavation of burnt mounds always reveals these troughs, and has produced evidence of hearths and fragments of bone and pottery. Sometimes mounds contain the remains of small house-like structures of stone and, more rarely, wood. Burnt mounds are often easy to locate, because their composition small refectories. It is interesting that in more southerly parts of Britain one of the first things to be made in bronze were large cauldrons, suggesting communal feasting: perhaps the burnt mound is Shetland's answer to the problem of how to cook enough for a feast with little fuel and no cauldron! It would be an interesting project to compare the distribution of burnt mounds (mainly in north and west Scotland) with the distribution of cauldrons and cauldron fragments and moulds (mainly in the east and south), to see if the two patterns overlap or are mutually exclusive.

Another possibility suggested for burnt mounds elsewhere in Britain has been as sites where cloth was processed, particularly for the fulling and/or the felting of woollen cloths. Although Shetland has a recent tradition of woollen manufacture, this is not an explanation of burnt mounds which much appeals to local opinion, to which perhaps archaeologists should listen more often than we tend to.

There is an even more exotic possibility for burnt mounds. Some have suggested that they are akin to saunas, and are primarily for bathing and cleansing. If this is correct, and some of the troughs in mounds are big enough to form respectable hip-baths, the abundance of domestic debris suggests that if these were saunas, they were saunas with snack-bars! Perhaps we should also recall that ritual bathing plays a significant role in the rituals of almost all present-day religions and not rule out the bathing hypothesis, hard as it may be to demonstrate from archaeological evidence.

Whatever is happening at burnt mounds, it seems to indicate a continuing tendency to gather together, to do things communally rather than in isolated family-sized groups. In the Neolithic, the chambered cairns indicate such collective enterprises. The small clusters of houses at Jarlshof and Sumburgh, together with the burnt mounds, are indicating something similar in the Bronze Age. It is a basic human instinct to gather together, at least from time to time. It also seems to be a basic instinct to feel the need for such gatherings to serve some higher purpose, be it religion, politics or sporting competition, to justify these naturally gregarious tendencies, rather than admitting that we just enjoy each other's company.

Stones on end

BEFORE moving on to the Iron Age, it is worth dwelling on the theme of collective enterprises to consider a group of monuments which are hard to place, both in time and in their significance to prehistoric Shetlanders.

Like many standing stones, this one at Skellister in Nesting has acquired a local name – "The Auld Wife" (52).

Like many parts of upland Britain, Shetland abounds in standing stones, often isolated but sometimes occurring in pairs or alignments. We know from excavations elsewhere that standing stones were erected at a wide range of dates, but the most

spectacular arrangements, the stone circles, seem to be of late Neolithic or early Bronze Age date. Not that all standing stones are Bronze Age by any means: upright stones make good navigation points and boundary markers, and doubtless have been placed for these purposes in later times – although of course genuinely prehistoric stones may later have been used for these purposes too.

Older reference books list a single stone circle in Shetland, but this sorry-looking site, on the slopes of Wormadale Hill in Tingwall, is almost certainly nothing more than the remains of the wall of a roughly circular field. There is nothing to compare with the two splendid rings in Orkney, at Stenness and Brodgar. But then, these impressive sites are exceptional in the whole of the north. Shetland is not without smaller circular settings which may be Bronze Age in date. On the moors of Fetlar, the puzzling Haltadans (36) consists of a ring of large blocks, not on end, surrounding a pair of large uprights. It looks as if it might have affinities with Bronze Age cairns more than with stone circles, as do the Rounds of Tivla on Unst (27), three sets of circular banks surrounding central stony areas.

There are other, more irregular enclosures of large boulders which do not seem to be agricultural, although these have yet to be tested by excavation – the best example is probably the Battle Pund on Out Skerries (42). One final type of stone setting, sets of "stone rows" were until recently harder to place in a Bronze Age context. These sites, most frequent in Caithness, each consist of several sub-parallel rows of short, stubby, upright stones. Shetland only has one reasonably convincing example, at Lumbister in Yell (34). Until recently, no stone-row site had been scientifically excavated, but now one has been examined in Caithness. Apart from confirming a Bronze Age date, the dig also reinforced the association of such rows with round burial cairns. But the Lumbister example is unique in Shetland, and may yet prove to be something completely different.

Most of the standing stones in Shetland are singletons or pairs. These are very hard to date, although some, perhaps most, doubtless go back to prehistoric times. The fact that a legend or a nickname has become attached to a stone over the centuries or that it features in a recent farm boundary or as a sailing mark for those at sea does not help with dating. Stones are prominent landmarks, and once upright may serve many purposes, from the focus of a good story to the key to relocating a good fishing area. Any upright stone is a useful feature in an area which, like Shetland, is often short of distinctive natural landmarks.

Some pairs of stones, especially if aligned up and down slope above the shore, may well have been erected to guide vessels in from the sea along a line with no dangerous rocks, or to give a bearing onto a fishing area. The pair at Clivocast in Unst (32) are a good example. Of course, pairs of stones are not needed to help with navigation – even a single stone which can be lined up with some horizon feature will do – the large stone at Busta (49) may fall into this category.

Close-set pairs of stones may, on the other hand, be the last remains of some otherwise vanished structure. At Housetter, beside the road to North Roe, is a much-ruined chambered cairn with two large uprights marking each end of its façade (43). It does not require much imagination to picture this cairn if stone-robbing had completed the removal of the remainder of the smaller stones – all that would be left would be a pair of upright stones standing a few metres

The age of some sites is shown by their influence on place names. This small standing stone must have been here before the establishment of the nearby croft, which is called Stanesland.

Stones on end

deeds which have attached themselves to standing stones, no burial has ever been found at the foot of one.

Rather than sites of prehistoric ritual or offshore navigation, the majority of standing stones in Shetland are probably no more than boundary markers, although this does not mean they are not ancient and important, especially if the ideas expressed earlier regarding the early date of Neolithic land division are valid. Boundary stones were certainly erected in medieval times as well. Such boundaries and markers may have had prehistoric protection long before they attracted biblical support ("cursed be he who moves another's boundary stone") or proverbial approval ("good fences make good neighbours").

Singleton standing stones will, for the most part, remain enigmatic. We can be sure only that they were erected for a wide variety of reasons at a wide variety of times. Even today, the urge to raise stones on end remains with us, as witness the examples beside stretches of recently reconstructed main road throughout Shetland. Fortunately for the archaeologist, these more modern examples tend to be inscribed with the date of their erection. If only our prehistoric ancestors had been so considerate!

Over the millennia, stones set up for other reasons have come to serve as sailing marks, and new stones have been erected just for that purpose – at Clivocast in Unst, overlooking the eastern approach to Uyeasound, either explanation might fit (31).

apart. At Wester Skeld (60) a set of polished stone knives was found buried close beside a standing stone – coincidence or marker? Oddly, despite the many stories of grisly

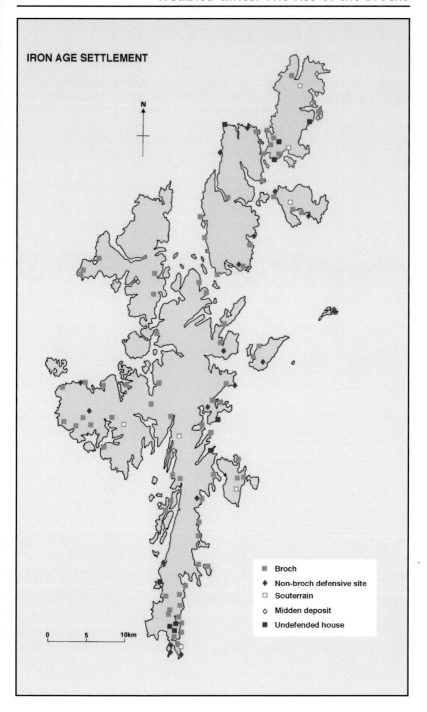

IRON AGE SETTLEMENT

N

■ Broch
◆ Non-broch defensive site
□ Souterrain
◇ Midden deposit
■ Undefended house

0   5   10km

Troubled times: The rise of the Brochs

THE MIDDLE centuries of the first millennium BC saw a major change in Shetland. From the unenclosed single farms of the Neolithic and earlier Bronze Age there had already evolved more nucleated settlements, with houses clustered together, often close to the shore, as at Jarlshof. As has been seen, there were good environmental reasons for this. But somewhere around this time a new factor emerged as a dominant theme: defence. This was to have a huge impact on many aspects of life in Shetland, and has left a range of superb archaeological sites.

As the population was probably steadily increasing, even though climatic change was reducing the capacity of the land to feed those people, it was inevitable that in Shetland, as elsewhere in northern Europe, the time would come when minor wrangles over territory would develop into longer lasting feuds, and feuds into localised warfare. To protect themselves from hostile neighbours, groups of families began to band together. At first these groupings would have been regarded as temporary measures, and defensive efforts would have been managed by the traditional heads of the community, who might perhaps have been religious leaders. But as time went on, these new arrangements became a permanent part of the structure of society. A new class of leaders emerged with skills more suited to direction and command, rather than co-ordination and consensus. These new leaders either appropriated or subordinated the old hierarchies based on religion and knowledge-bearing.

This reorganisation of commun-ities into larger units with stronger internal ties and more assertive and ambitious leaders, which must have meant some loss of individual freedom in return for security, transcended its original purpose. Although communities did, indeed, become better able to defend themselves against external attack, the new social structure ultimately led to more instability, for it also facilitated hostile activities. Raids and land-takings became much easier for aggressive and newly-powerful leaders to mount, and a downward spiral of insecurity set in, requiring ever greater defensive preparations. It has even been suggested that society became strongly militarised at this time. Such a process of conflict escalation and militarisation is not unfamiliar in much more recent times, of course.

It would be naïve to imagine that such major changes happened in Shetland in isolation, and indeed the first signs of defensive constructions appear to lie close in time to the arrival of new styles of pottery, new bronze ornaments and, perhaps most important, a new metal: iron. There has been much debate as to how these new ideas, and the idea of defensive building, reached Shetland. Some would see the entire "Iron Age package" arriving from the south, presumably Orkney, with the new-style leaders – warlords – being immigrant aristocrats who controlled the new technology very closely. Others see these changes being introduced as ideas adopted by the local population, with no incomers at all, although no-one nowadays argues that everything originated in Shetland without reference to the outside world. This,

in many ways, is the same invasion versus local adaptation argument as at the start of the Neolithic, although there is a significant difference: if our reading of Iron Age society is correct, it is much easier to imagine a true invasion – a military conquest – at this time than 3000 years earlier.

The archaeological evidence is equivocal. At Clickimin (21a), there appears to already be a simple fort in existence before iron-working appears, but at Jarlshof (25a) the reverse is true. Meanwhile at Wiltrow iron-working appears to be compatible with a simple prehistoric house, suggesting that it was not closely identified with fortified sites.

It is interesting to note that in Ireland and in France, where we have more evidence of these matters in the Iron Age, it is not so much the production of iron and bronze which is controlled by the higher echelons of society as the production of precious metals and jewellery. There is some evidence that smiths – of iron in particular – had a social status akin to that which they still enjoy in some less industrial societies today, a position of respect but one slightly apart from society, as servants of a useful, but suspect, quasi-magical process. (Everybody respects iron-smiths, but they do not want their daughter to marry one.) In many recent societies, iron seems to have been regarded as special in a way which bronze does not – perhaps because of the more complex processes needed to extract it from its ores.

We can safely state that iron reached Shetland at much the same time that society was reorganising itself all over northern Europe, and that this social reorganisation made major projects of defensive construction both necessary and

At the start of the Iron Age, houses continued to be built in traditional style, although tending to be a little smaller than their earlier counterparts. This small late Bronze Age or early Iron Age example which pre-dates the broch at Clickimin has been partially restored (21).

Troubled times: The rise of the Brochs

feasible, the results of which have come down to us the many ruins of forts and brochs throughout Shetland. But did the social changes lead to the need for defence, or did the need for defence lead to the social changes? That is where theory takes over from observation. The Iron Age, and especially the Iron Age of the broch-building areas such as Shetland, is bedevilled with theories, ranging from the "collective heroic defence of the homeland" or "fully-fledged military society" at one end of the spectrum, through the "sensible precaution against unlikely hostilities" in the middle to the "purely for prestige purposes" at the opposite end. It is interesting to reflect that theories tend to align with the political leanings of those doing the theorising – but much more interesting to consider the evidence, and decide for ourselves.

There is relatively little evidence for the beginnings of the Iron Age in Shetland, which is unfortunate, since

the seeds of major changes in the middle of this period must have been laid in the years from about 700 to 300 BC. We know that iron was introduced in this period, but have not so far identified any iron-working sites much earlier than 300 BC. It seems a reasonable proposition that the majority of people continued a lifestyle which was essentially an extension of the Neolithic-Bronze Age one, except that almost everyone was now living close to the coast, with the higher hill slopes used only for grazing. We assume, because it was at this period that climatic deterioration reached its worst before beginning a slow recovery, that the farming economy was more strongly tilted towards pastoral activities and away from arable than at any other time in the prehistoric period.

But when it comes to finding actual sites to back up these assumptions, there are few. The only excavated sites with remains which date firmly to the early Iron Age are Jarlshof (25a) (where several relatively slightly-built circular houses were in use at this time), possibly the earliest defensive structure at Clickimin (21a), and a group of small but otherwise unremarkable prehistoric houses at Mavis Grind. In addition, the use of an earlier house at Wiltrow as a smith's workshop also dates to this period. One site per century is not much on which to build a reliable picture.

Doubtless there are other sites of this date, but they have yet to be recognised. If people continued to live in houses not dissimilar to those of earlier times, except perhaps a little smaller and more closely clustered together on low ground near the shore, this might explain why we have not so far spotted many. Another factor must be that after this period arable cultivation seems to have expanded again in extent, and during this expansion the stones of late Bronze Age-early Iron Age house ruins may have been removed for use in field walls and to release scarce land for cultivation.

By contrast, Shetland has a positive wealth of archaeological sites dating to the middle part of the

Iron Age, from around 300 BC (although that date is constantly under revision as research progresses) to around AD 150. This abundance is not because there was a sudden population boom, but because this period was marked by the construction of very large and complex stone structures. These were so substantial that after their period of currency ended it was seldom worth the effort to remove them.

These massive middle Iron Age structures, especially the brochs – a spectacular achievement of prehistoric architecture, unique to Scotland, of which Shetland has the finest surviving example in the Broch of Mousa – have attracted more study than any other aspect of Shetland's prehistory. While this means that we have more information about this period than any other comparable span of prehistory, we also realise just how much we do not know. Bland generalisations are clearly in-adequate, but we lack precise answers for many of our detailed questions.

It is often thought that the only type of fortified structure in prehistoric Shetland is the broch, a

Walls and ramparts around brochs may have been earlier than the brochs themselves: this was the case at Clickimin (21a).

Simple forts, such as that at Burga Water on the Sandness road, may be earlier than brochs or they may simply be "poor relations" (101).

Promontory forts such as Landberg on Fair Isle make use of natural cliffs to economise on building. Only a few short stretches of ditch and bank provide a substantial enclosed area (111)...

...with a spectacular view of Sheep Rock: but what was it like in stormy weather? It is hard to believe that such sites were permanently occupied.

tall circular fort of drystone construction, with a thick, hollow wall and a single small entrance. But in fact there are quite a number of other types, though mainly on a more modest scale. Some of these look as if they pre-date brochs, particularly at the excavated site of Clickimin (21a), where a defensive wall was built and modified a number of times before a broch was built on the same site. We do not know if all of the smaller forts pre-date brochs: the patchy evidence suggests that some, at least, may be contemporary with them.

Non-broch forts in Shetland occupy two kinds of location: cliffed promontories and small islands in lochs or sheltered inlets of the sea. They are economical in construction: a substantial area can be enclosed by running a short stretch of wall or rampart and a ditch across a narrow neck of land, while an islet can be given a relatively slight circuit if its only approach is along a narrow causeway. It is noticeable that both promontory forts and islet forts (which would be called "duns" in the Gaelic speaking parts of Scotland) often have quite elaborate gateways facing the likely line of landward approach and rather unimpressive walls around the rest of the site – this may be seen well at Clickimin (21a) or at Loch of Huxter (96).

Elsewhere, defences are simpler – from one to three earthen banks would be thrown up across a promontory, with intervening ditches, and a single gap which was presumably closed by a wooden gate. These forts tend to enclose tiny areas of land, and are often themselves of modest stature – individual banks and ditches seldom having an amplitude of more than three metres. Good examples of such simple promontory forts occur at Aywick (92), Ness of Garth (100) and at Hog Island (99): the last two show the effects of rising sea-level, which has cut through what were probably dry ditches to create in one case a tidal, and in the other case a permanently flooded, moat. Forts which appear to be simple are not always so, and recent excavation of supposedly simple forts at Landberg (111) and Scatness North (109) revealed rectangular masonry gateways, or "blockhouses" as they are sometimes termed, similar to that at Ness of Burgi (110).

Nor is the purpose of these forts clearly understood. Some, at least, are quite well located to be bridgeheads of some invading force, but equally others look almost like "poor man's brochs", stuck in out of the way and not very fertile locations on upland lochs or "lookout stations" on exposed cliff edges. We lack dates for the construction of these sites, but at a guess we may, indeed, be looking at several different situations. Some of the forts may genuinely be early, perhaps even the first toe-hold of incomers intent on carving out a new life in Shetland. If successful, succeeding generations might have held such places in special esteem – one thinks of Plymouth Rock in America. Others may, indeed, have been the strongholds of those whose neighbours built brochs, but who could not quite amass the resources or labour needed to copy them. And a few may have been lookout points, or perhaps prominent warnings to anyone approaching by sea that the land behind was already taken.

All of the excavated forts contain some features typical of brochs, but in the absence of dating we cannot say if this is because they were ancestral and contain ideas later to be fully developed in brochs, or on the other hand contemporary and drawn from the same architectural

vocabulary, but for a different purpose. Were they all even forts as we understand that term: defensive structures? It has been suggested that some of the larger rectangular "blockhouse" forts, such as Ness of Burgi, were nothing more than massive "posing platforms" for Iron Age warriors to display their martial ardour without actually engaging in combat. But such ideas, which have also been aired for the brochs, go further than present-day archaeological skills can take us.

There is an overlap between these forts and the brochs themselves.

Erosion has changed many sites, as at Scatness North. The outer ramparts and a fragment of blockhouse can be seen, but the area enclosed has vanished, along with half the blockhouse (109).

On the next headland south is Ness of Burgi, where there has been less erosion and the form of the blockhouse is very clear (110).

Brochs were not built by people who wished to hide away from public view, as the skyline setting of Culswick emphasises (102).

Almost half of Shetland's broch sites have walls, ramparts or ditches around them, and many of these would have been classed as forts if they did not have brochs within them. The outer defences of broch sites such as Burland (104), Aithsetter and Burraland would make respectable promontory forts, while Culswick (102) and Southpunds have very fine walls around them, like the early fort at Clickimin (21a). Massive earthen ramparts around Underhoull (88), Belmont (89) and Dalsetter (107) are more impressive than the tumbled broch ruins within them. With the sole exception of Jarlshof (25a), every excavation which has produced a sequence has shown that the outer wall or ramparts pre-dated the broch, although not necessarily by long. These may be old forts re-fitted with brochs, or they may be broch sites temporarily protected by quickly-built temporary fortifications: we just do not know.

The whole question of the origin and purpose of brochs has attracted more ink than any other aspect of Scottish prehistory. The fact that they are a building type unique to Scotland, coupled with their remarkable architectural sophistication, has doubtless helped promote their iconic status, with the Broch of Mousa as the icon of icons.

Mousa (105) is the best preserved broch of all. A circular foundation 4.5 metres thick surrounds an inner courtyard six metres across. This massive foundation is pierced by an

At some broch sites, the outer ramparts are the most impressive survival – Dalsetter near Boddam (107).

entrance passage one metre wide with a recess part-way along the passage, in which would have been set the frame for a wooden door. Within the solid base of the wall are three oval rooms, or "cells" with corbelled roofs. These are accessed from the inner courtyard by narrow doorways. At a height of three metres, the character of the broch's tall wall changes, becoming a double-skinned hollow construction, the inner and outer faces tied together by six levels of long lintel stones, creating "galleries" within the wall. A steep stone stairway spirals upwards within this hollow wall, cutting each gallery in turn before emerging at the wall-head, 13 metres above ground level. All of this was achieved in drystone masonry, without any lime or mortar.

There is evidence from several brochs for wooden internal arrangements, and most archaeologists believe that every broch's inner courtyard was fitted out with wooden buildings, including one or more raised floors, supported on stout posts and on the ledges which project from the inner face of the broch's wall. These wooden buildings and the roof have in every case long vanished, but would have meant that brochs were comfortable and spacious, capable of housing a chiefly family in style or accommodating the whole local population at times of crisis.

Mousa looks almost too good to be true, but there seems to be no truth in the often-heard story that it is a 19th century reconstruction, although it was certainly repaired around 1851. It was still well-enough preserved in the 11th

century to serve as shelter for Norse fugitives, an event chronicled in the sagas, where it was described as "an unhandy place to get at".

Mousa is not quite typical of brochs. Enough survives at many of Shetland's other broch sites, 75 to 80 in number, to tell us that Mousa is smaller in diameter and more

Mousa stands over 13m tall, the epitome of "broch-ness". It commands a view over the passage between the island and the mainland shore, where another broch is located (105).

Inside, Mousa shows ladder-like apertures called "voids", which reduce the weight of the structure and allow light and air to penetrate into the galleries. It is believed the interiors of brochs were occupied by galleried wooden structures (105).

Troubled times: The rise of the Brochs

we would call an "architectural statement".

Yet there is little doubt that most brochs were tall enough to be described as towers. (By all but the true pedant, that is, who requires a tower to be taller than it is wide. On this criterion, even Mousa fails!) Mousa also lacks the typical "guard cells" found in so many brochs. These are small oval chambers in the wall-base, opening into the side of the entrance passage just behind the doorway. Guard cells are so-called because they are usually presumed to be for the positioning of a door-keeper, or at least a fierce dog or two. But they might just have been convenient places to stow wet or messy possessions, in effect prehistoric porches. Above the roof lintels of the entrance passage, some brochs such as Clickimin had a chamber in the wall through which the defenders could look down on those entering – and presumably poke them with spears if necessary.

At Clickimin, voids appear above the entrance passage. Perhaps the level immediately above the passage allowed those entering to be secretly inspected – and if necessary disposed of (21a).

Typically the door of a broch was set half-way down the passage. The stone jambs, against which the wooden door-frame would have fitted, can be seen here at Clickimin (21a).

massive in construction than the rest. Having a thicker wall in proportion to the overall diameter than any other, it could have been built taller than average, and Mousa may be the tallest broch ever built. Indeed, its height seems to be excessive, and not to add much to its defensibility – given the military technology of the time (spears, bows and arrows, battering rams) there is no obvious reason why a 13 metre tower is better for defence than a 10 metre tower, or even a seven metre one. There is a feeling about Mousa that it is almost a demonstration piece, flaunting the skills of the builders and the status of the owners – what in modern jargon

Most brochs in Shetland had a number of lesser buildings around them. It may be that these were built at the same time as the broch, and designed from the start to function as part of a single complex with the broch tower. This has been argued for the site of Gurness in Orkney, for example. But most external buildings give the impression of later "overflow" housing, an impression confirmed at the large-scale excavations recently concluded at Old Scatness (108). Brochs were in some cases built on sites which were already occupied, as at Clickimin (21a) and Jarlshof (25a), but their construction seems to have more or less ignored what came before, with the exception of defensive ramparts

or ditches. As already discussed, some of these outer defences may have been created before brochs were built. The usefulness of outer defences seems to end quite soon after brochs were erected, for it is common – in Shetland and beyond – to find later Iron Age houses built over infilled ditches and levelled ramparts.

The largest of these settlements around brochs coincide with areas of good farmland, as might be expected. Were the occupants of the lesser buildings serfs or slaves to the broch-owners? Or was the whole complex a relatively egalitarian arrangement, with the broch built and used communally by families who, after throwing up the broch in an initial panic, re-assessed the degree of threat and decided it was

safe to build individual houses around the broch rather than continue living cheek-by-jowl inside the barrack-like tower?

Brochs are large and complicated structures, and the complexes around them add to this complexity. Modern archaeology is slow, painstaking and expensive. So it is rare for a complete "broch village" to be excavated. Shetland is fortunate in this respect, with the huge excavation – the most costly single excavation project to date in Scotland – at Old Scatness (108), over ten years from 1995. This has added hugely to our detailed knowledge of Iron Age Shetland, and the analysis of the huge array of finds and the detailed histories of houses will soon provide a uniquely detailed picture of life in the

Some brochs which lay in fertile farmland quickly became surrounded by a clutter of other buildings, as here at Jarlshof: not ideal for defence (25a).

Troubled times: The rise of the Brochs

centuries around the BC/AD divide. It may even allow us to come closer to an answer to such tantalising questions as that posed in the previous paragraph. It would be unfair (and dangerous) to pre-judge the results, but some important information already announced requires us to adjust our way of looking at brochs and the middle Iron Age.

The most significant fact is that the broch was almost certainly built in the period 300-200 BC. This parallels recent construction dates from a broch in the Outer Hebrides, and requires a major re-think of broch origins. It is not possible to contemplate the origins of brochs without at the same time trying to understand their purpose.

What were brochs for? Once thought of as Viking watch-towers,

Broch-builders used whatever material came to hand, and there is no evidence that they carried stone for any distance to build better. The awkward red granite at Culswick was adequate for the purpose, although it does not form regular slabs or blocks (102).

or watch-towers of the local people against the Vikings, they have long been known to be much earlier in date. At one time they were thought to be the homes of immigrant Celtic landlords, driven into the far north and west by population movements arising in southern and central Europe at much the same time as the Roman Empire began to expand. The broch idea was held to have been brought north by such people – even though there are no brochs or anything like them in the areas of southern and western England whence they were supposed to have come.

Latterly, brochs have generally been interpreted as the fortified homes of local chieftains who were defending themselves and their extended family against raids either from neighbours or from outside the islands. But once again, the context was the backwash of the Roman expansion through Europe. It was suggested that life was troubled, sporadic raiding was common and those captured in such raids became slaves, either bearing the children, working the farmland and rowing the ships of those who took them, or else being sold on as a commodity into the Roman Empire. So brochs were, essentially, "people-safes". The new, earlier dating for the start of broch-building, around 300 BC, removes the idea of the Roman expansion as the ultimate cause of the social unrest and as a market – at least to begin with – of any slaves. We must now look for more local reasons behind the building of brochs.

As an architectural entity, the broch seems to be a highly standardised idea, but one which allows some flexibility of dimensions and layout. The ideas which go to make up a broch all seem to have been present in northern and western Scotland: circularity in the widespread hut circles and especially in some very heavily-walled examples of these in parts of Sutherland and Orkney; hollow walls in the duns of the west coast and the blockhouse forts of Shetland; elaborate gateways also in the Shetland blockhouse forts and the galleried duns of the West Coast and the Hebrides. Nowadays no-one doubts that the broch is a Scottish invention, an amalgam of pre-existing ideas.

But argument still simmers over where the first "true" broch (tower with hollow wall and specialised doorway) was created. In the days when all broch-building had to be fitted into the last century BC and the first century AD, this was a vital quest, because only a single point of invention followed by a very rapid spread could account for over 500 brochs scattered from the Mull of Galloway to the northern tip of Unst. The rival claims of Skye and the Inner Hebrides and Orkney or Caithness were fiercely and ingeniously advocated by different academic coteries. But as the new, earlier, dates for some brochs have come forward, including dates for crude structures which might be broch ancestors in Orkney as early as 600 BC, it has become much more reasonable to suppose that the broch was not invented in any one place, but arose out of a process of evolution and sharing of innovations. There was clearly a desire to perfect a structure which was both defensive and impressive,

and this gradually homed in on what today we call the broch – in much the same way as most modern cars have evolved to look rather like one another. Functional needs (and perhaps fashionable fads) combined to make the broch the "must-have" building for the "happening community".

This view of gradual evolution requires the broch to have served its purpose well. If its purpose was defensive, to protect against sudden attack, it is hard to imagine the entire livestock of a community being driven inside through the single narrow entrance – although only too easy to imagine the chaos inside if this were done. On the other hand, the broch would have been a relatively good strongpoint in which valuables – perhaps grain and dairy produce – could have been placed, along with the non-fighting members of the populace, while the fighting men (and women?) drove off any attackers. Everyone simply shutting themselves inside and hoping trouble would go away seems altogether unlikely as a technique of defence, since any attackers could simply take possession of land and cattle and, keeping out of stone, spear or arrow range, wait for their foes to emerge from the broch. Use of a broch as a temporary bolthole might work if there was a pre-arranged system of signals (smoke or fire) to summon help from neighbouring settlements – and if the neighbours were willing to help.

All of these scenarios envisage lightly armed raiding parties of no very large size, adequate to defeat the people living in and around any one broch, but not sufficiently

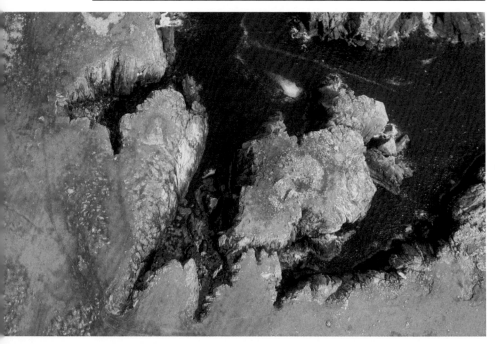

Broch ruins on the island of Balta, off Unst. Such exposed, isolated, brochs probably served as lookout posts and warning signals, perhaps only seasonally manned. When their utility ceased, there was no incentive to remain. Photo: Mike Brooks.

strong to take on several such groups if they banded together. Some academics have gone so far as to suggest such raids were in effect "sport" rather than war, although a very cruel sport by modern standards. We can be fairly sure that prolonged sieges were not expected: many brochs have no permanent water supply, and when the Romans eventually reached these parts, their heavy siege gear would have made rubble of a broch in short order.

Recently, several different ideas about how brochs fitted into society have been developed. It now seems to be generally agreed that broch society was hierarchical and that not everyone expected to live in a broch tower. (It is notable that older ideas about group ownership and community effort seem to have faded as communism has lost

ground worldwide in recent years, much as ideas about invasion and military conquest became outmoded as the world moved further in time from the last World War.) Such views all require an explanation of where everyone else lived. The absence of much evidence for contemporary non-broch settlement is attributed to the use of turf or wood, rather than stone, as building materials, or to the remains of ordinary farmhouses of this period lying below later settlements.

If the rather large problem of where everyone else lived is put to one side, here are three current ideas about how brochs fitted into society:

♦ They were the "manor-farms" of each district, occupied by gentleman farmers who ran their own agricultural enterprises (probably with slave or serf labour), collected rents in kind from other small farms and organised any trade into or out of the district. These "lairds" (to use the Scots term) also indulged in illicit activities such as cattle-stealing, and therefore had to be able to defend themselves, their families and their retainers in case of reprisals. The scale of the structure signals the importance of the owner – one is only a gentleman farmer if one can manage to build a broch.

♦ They were storage and distribution points for surplus food, particularly grain, acquired by a regular levy on crops and used for trade and to buffer the population against bad harvests. Brochs, on this argument, represent the warehouses and dwelling-places of chieftains who controlled society through control over commodities. The strong broch structure was partly to deter those who wish to take food without "payment" – although what form payment takes, in a currency-free society, is a moot point – and partly to show the wealth of its owner. This is essentially a development of the "manor-house" argument, but takes it a step towards collective farming.

♦ They were part of a planned system of territorial domination and defence against external attack, built by the leaders of a society which, rather like the later Zulu nation, was militarised in all essential aspects of its organisation. Such a society might have evolved locally as a means of retaining control in the face of rising population

numbers, scarce food supplies, and increased immigration from elsewhere. Alternatively it might have been imposed on reluctant Shetlanders by the leaders of a successful conquest from outside Shetland – perhaps from Orkney or Caithness.

The first two theories are not mutually inconsistent, and are essentially developments of the current orthodoxy that brochs are fortified farmhouses, viewed according to two different models of how the top-level of the agricultural economy was managed. But they fail adequately to explain why some brochs are sited in places which are useless for arable agriculture – unless the brochs on exposed cliff-tops were storing smoked gannets, pickled guillemot-eggs or similar – not impossible, perhaps, but unlikely.

A unifying view of these two theories asserts that a broch is simply what the "top" family in any middle Iron Age neighbourhood builds, that its form may have defensive origins but is by now really about social prestige, and that it is built at a location where the resources of any "territory" can be exploited efficiently, be they arable, pastoral or marine. Those who live in territories which are poor for arable production make up for it by trading with neighbouring groups for what they lack.

The third theory is a reworking of an old idea which was rejected long ago, when it became clear that brochs were not defensive strongpoints against Viking attack. But it has recently been revived in an updated form and its proponents – so far few but wily – point to the way in which brochs seem to be distributed to "hold" every area of land along the coastline, especially against attack from the sea; the standardised construction, to a mental if not an actual blueprint, the extreme effort involved for simple agricultural communities to build brochs and the asserted (but not proven) fact that all Shetland's brochs are built over a short timescale.

Following this theory, which is certainly worth serious consideration, it may be that an immigrant military hierarchy dominated the unwilling populace in every aspect of life, forcing them to build and maintain brochs as defensive strongpoints – even though these might only have to be manned by fighting men during the summer season, the only time when any new invasion might be expected. Equally, it might be that, either through invasion or by evolution, society had developed a military organisation which pervaded every aspect of life, perhaps because there was a perception of some great threat which only such a regimented lifestyle could avert. This might be an external threat, such as invasion, an internal threat, such as famine, or something more esoteric, such as a fear of social chaos if "the old ways" were dispensed with. Military dictatorships throughout the ages have justified their actions in many ways, and always "for the good of the people".

As was said above, we know so much about brochs that we can build ever more elaborate theories. Every new excavation provides fresh evidence which can be interpreted in many ways. Archaeologists are clearly in no danger of running out of ideas!

The fall of the Brochs: Peace, Picts and Priests

WHATEVER scenario one chooses to explain the large numbers of brochs and forts in Shetland, two facts emerge. The first is that people continued to farm, to fish and to live their everyday lives. The second is that, after a time, brochs stopped being built and maintained. Until recently, neither of these facts has been afforded much attention by broch-bedazzled researchers.

Until the recent excavations at Old Scatness (108), and also at Upper Scalloway, our knowledge of the domestic and agricultural side of the broch period was based on evidence from older excavations, especially at Jarlshof (25a). While these earlier digs took place to an excellent standard for their day, they did not systematically recover such a wide range of evidence about diet – for example only larger bones and fragments of wood were recovered. Modern excavations descend to the microscopic level to recover pollen, seeds, fragments of insects, the tiniest of animal, bird and fish bones and even human and animal droppings – all of these can help to provide a picture of conditions on and around sites.

While the detailed results have yet to be published, some very interesting facts are emerging. Study of soils around Old Scatness has provided evidence for systematic soil management, with the addition of basic ash and animal manure to enrich the soil and counter acidity. There also seems to have been a very substantial grain component in the diet – although this site is in one of the best areas of Shetland for crop-raising – rather contradicting the previous view that Iron Age Shetlanders relied heavily on dairy

produce, meat and fish. Of course, it might be that diet was differentiated according to class, but it would be an odd society in which the top class (in the broch and its surrounding houses) ate bread while the lower class had a high protein diet!

There is much more investigation to be done, and every dig always has the problem that what is found on the site, even in a total excavation, is not necessarily representative of the norm. In the Iron Age, as today, certain types of refuse would have been disposed of in different ways, some being recycled and much being composted for use as agricultural fertiliser. It is also worth considering what effect ritual processing of food and linked taboos might have on the patterns of deposition: it is perfectly possible that something akin to modern "kosher" or "hallal" practices might have operated in the Iron Age. Bones of certain species seem to be present in great numbers at some periods and absent at others. The seal, both grey and common, is a striking example – do the "silkie" tales of recent folklore reflect a much older special attitude to these creatures?

Eventually, as at Old Scatness (seen during the 2002 excavation season) a broch might be reduced in height and become buried in later structures. Here the broch is the large curving wall to the left of the photograph. When emptied, it was found still to stand well over 3m tall (108).

It was not only architecture that changed: rotary querns were a technological improvement that came into Britain from continental Europe during the middle Iron Age. This elaborate example is from the excavations at Bayanne.

What tends to survive on site are objects which are not useful for any further purpose. Stone querns (grinders for grain) are typical finds – at first simple trough or saddle querns, with the rotary quern appearing not long after the brochs themselves. When these are broken, they tend to be incorporated into wall or floor repairs. Large animal bones often survive, possibly

identified a very large range of species, particularly birds, with everything from great auk (individuals larger than any surviving museum specimens of this now-extinct flightless bird) to crane to black grouse. The last two species point out a problem with using excavation evidence to re-create past natural environments: did they live in Shetland, or were they brought in as bones or carcases? The long, hollow bones of the crane are still used in other parts of the world to make flutes, while a brace of well-hung black grouse (a woodland species) would perhaps have been a suitable gift for a visitor to bring with him from, say, Aberdeenshire.

Another way of considering the Iron Age economy is to look at local geography – where brochs were sited relative to the natural landscape and the resources it would have provided. This method, which has been applied to Shetland's brochs with some appearance of success, suggests that brochs were established in an economy based on mixed agriculture, with as much arable land for grain as could be brought into cultivation by careful soil management (aided by a stabilisation in the climatic conditions from their previous long deterioration), coupled to pastoral activity, with cattle more important than sheep, with dairying rather than meat-production the main goal. We assume, but cannot demonstrate, that fishing and the use of coastal resources remained important.

Rotary quern: in all essential aspects, this technology remained unchanged for almost 2000 years. Southvoe Croft Museum.

because they were set aside for future use in making bone tools, and frequently heaps of shellfish remains – limpets in particular, perhaps for fishing bait rather than as a direct source of food. Analysis of bones from the Jarlshof excavations

But of course what has just been described is essentially how Shetlanders lived until the 19th century AD, what we would now refer to as a crofting lifestyle. Even if brochs were not farmhouses, there is no reason to suppose that the economy was substantially different from that depicted here – it is simply the most productive system which the nature of Shetland and its resources combined with the technology of the period would allow. It is striking how almost every broch ruin seems to be in an area which in more recent times supported about six to 10 croft holdings (sometimes more), and this casual observation helps to explain, for those who do not believe brochs were farmhouses, why we cannot find many middle Iron Age dwellings – their remains would lie under the floors of more recent crofts. Even the remains of Iron Age fields are hard to find, surviving only at a few broch sites in locations which were marginal then and have remained so since: Burra Ness (91) and Greenbank in Yell have lines of walling and field clearance cairns nearby which are probably of the broch period.

The second indisputable fact about this period is that, probably in the late 1st or early 2nd century AD, brochs stopped being built and maintained. Some were reduced in height and converted from towers into more cosy single-storey farmsteads, while others were allowed to fall down, occasionally plundered for stone to build houses nearby. Some of Shetland's brochs were replaced by very distinctive dwellings called wheelhouses, but these were very different in character from the brochs, having none of the brochs' impressive stature or forbidding external appearance. There is very little evidence for

exactly when brochs ceased to be built and maintained. Although there are a few down in the Scottish Lowlands, well outside the main "broch province", which may only have been built as late as the first century AD, it is generally assumed that brochs went out of use some time in the early years of the AD era. The cessation of broch-building remains as large a problem for archaeology as the start. If anything, there are too many possible explanations, all of them conditioned by which view one takes of the primary purpose of brochs, and whether that purpose changed over time.

If brochs were essentially home-grown defences against local inter-community strife, or slave-taking, they might have been abandoned whether they failed or succeeded. A broch was a huge investment of effort for what was essentially a crofting community, even if driven or organised by strong leaders and a sense of fear. It is possible that the brochs were all built in a great rush of enthusiasm as "the ultimate deterrent" but that after a few had been successfully attacked and shown not to be effective defences, people lost faith in static defences and just accepted the risk of skirmishes on open ground. Or brochs may have succeeded totally, and by making each community proof against attack, removed the profitability of raiding, allowing a watchful but essentially peaceful life to continue until such time as the old rugged lifestyle was gradually forgotten. A similar pair of opposites would apply if brochs are seen as a planned military network: they either allowed Shetland to be held

The fall of the Brochs: Peace, Picts and Priests

More lightly built circular wheelhouses, so-called because of their radial stone piers, follow brochs on some sites in Shetland, as here at Old Scatness. These structures are common to Shetland and the Hebrides – in the Hebrides they may be contemporary with brochs and not later as in Shetland. So far no example has been found in Orkney, despite much excavation there (108).

by its defenders, or they failed, to be ignored or slighted by the victors. Or a revolution of downtrodden Shetland serfs may have unseated the hypothetical alien military overlords. The final possibility is that events far from Shetland – perhaps the *Pax Romana* – may have removed whatever external threat was the stimulus for broch-building. Only one fact is certain: some time before the mid 2nd century AD, Shetland's brochs – and apparently defences of any sort – came to be regarded as redundant.

If the answer to the sudden end of the brochs is a conscious decision taken, all across the area with brochs, that they were no longer needed – or were no longer acceptable – it must be said that such a decision would take effect much faster if there was some form of integrated command structure, rather than if each broch was the spontaneous creation of an individual landlord or local community. Therefore the date and

details of the circumstances of the abandonment of brochs, as indicated by their structural modification or the onset of neglect of maintenance, must be a target for future research.

Although archaeology can do little to throw direct light on the immediate social and political reasons for the demise of the brochs, it can tell us what followed them, and in this there are clues which support the idea of radical changes in social organisation and a marked increase in contacts with the outside world. We will return to the end of the brochs shortly, because it may have links to another problem – the appearance of the Picts.

On every broch site which has been investigated, the broch was replaced by lower, more modest houses, sometimes set into the ruined stump of the broch, sometimes built alongside it. Interestingly, in Shetland these groups of houses tend not to be large in number, and even at Old

Scatness it appears that no more than four or five were in use at any one time. This might indicate that broch sites remained high-status places, even when their primary role ended, and were still in the hands of the top families in local society. It has been suggested that wider Iron Age society changed at this time, from one in which dominance and/or prestige were expressed through monumental architecture to one in which status was expressed through displays of wealth, such as feasting, gift-exchange and personal adornment.

Jarlshof's wheelhouses were later buried in sand, and survived to roof height, affording a rare opportunity to enter an almost complete Iron Age dwelling (25b).

The post-broch period was not necessarily a slump, more of a "peace dividend" perhaps. Some of the architecture which replaced brochs in Shetland was just as sophisticated in its construction. The wheelhouse, for example, was a spacious circular house, with a tall internal space divided by well-built piers of stone radiating in from the wall towards a circular central hearth area. The piers divided the floor space into rooms for sleeping and living, and could be roofed by corbelling over in stone. The whole structure was encased within a solid but externally undistinguished stone shell and roofed over with a domed thatch roof. Wheelhouses were probably very comfortable, as the well-preserved examples at Jarlshof (25a) demonstrate, and the form was a much more sensible, wind-proof building style than the exposed and draughty broch. Wheelhouse-style architecture was also used away from former broch sites, as at Bayanne in Yell, supporting the idea of a population gradually spreading out from its former defensive centres.

Simpler houses also had architectural features reminiscent of wheelhouses. Excavation of an Iron Age house at Bayanne in Yell.

Having said that the post-broch period was not a slump, as generations went by houses did tend to become progressively smaller, as Old Scatness and Jarlshof both demonstrate. Wheelhouses were generally replaced by small round-houses, sometimes called aisled roundhouses because they share the piers of the wheelhouses, except that these were not joined to the inside face of the circular wall, but instead had small gaps or "aisles" between them and the wall. The evidence from Jarlshof shows that the first wheelhouses there came later than an aisled round house, but at Old Scatness the two types seem to have co-existed, although the wheelhouse form died out sooner. This trend from larger to smaller dwellings might be because a practice of communal living, begun with the brochs, was finally breaking down into life as individual family

The fall of the Brochs: Peace, Picts and Priests

units, or it might mark a real deterioration in quality of architecture and with it quality of life: we will return to this point a little later.

At the same time as brochs became redundant and wheelhouses and aisled roundhouses were being built and lived in, evidence appears from changing pottery styles and some other artefacts, such as Roman glass, of a much wider range of external contacts – with Orkney, perhaps the Hebrides (which also has wheelhouses, so far undetected in Orkney), the Scottish Mainland and possibly even with continental Europe. Whether these finds represent the arrival of new people – as conquerors or settlers – or simply an opening up of the islands to external contacts after a long period of defensive isolation, we cannot be sure.

It is tempting to picture a rosy post-conflict economic boom in which trade flourished and new links and friendships were established around the North Sea and the Atlantic seaboard, perhaps under the benevolent guard of the Roman navy. But this is also the period at which Shetland, along with Orkney, Caithness and Sutherland, begins to find its cultural identity progressively merged with the rest of northern Scotland, so it may not have been a totally carefree time.

By the middle of the first millennium AD, life in Shetland seems to have returned in some ways to how things were before the brochs. We had very few excavated sites of this period until the recent dig at Old Scatness. It looks as if this site is confirming the previous impression, that the elaborate wheelhouses which succeeded the

Late Iron Age houses tended to become simpler, like this one at Jarlshof (25b).

By the time the Iron Age is being referred to as Pictish, houses tend to be simple or composite oval plans, sometimes touchingly referred to as "jelly-baby" houses. Old Scatness (108).

spectacular brochs were also a passing phase, and over time houses tended to be smaller, circular or oval in plan, and often hard to distinguish on plan alone from those of earlier times.

However, there were some distinctly different architectural forms appearing in both Orkney and Shetland in the period around 500 AD. One was a lightly-built house, often set into the rubble of earlier buildings, possessing one main room with a large central hearth and a small inner room opening off it, at the opposite end from the external doorway. Because of their appearance on plan, these are known, depending upon the sensibilities of the archaeologist involved, as "figure-of-eight", "ventral" or "jelly-baby" houses. A good example may be seen at Jarlshof. It is also at this time that the earth-houses or souterrains appear in the north. Narrow sunken passages with larger chambers at their innermost ends, these mysterious structures were once regarded as defensive bolt-holes or religious shrines, but were probably no more than storage places, perhaps cool houses for dairy produce. They almost always seem to have been lain below or alongside above-ground round houses. There are not many souterrains in Shetland, and all of them are small by Scottish standards. They seem to be quite late here, whereas further south in Scotland – for example in Perthshire – some have been dated back to the earlier part of the Iron Age.

In local parlance, souterrains were "Picts' Hooses", and the time has come to introduce that supposedly mysterious people. Who were the Picts? Many books have been written and archaeological and historical careers carved out of that simple question, so it is dangerous ground on which to tread. But dangerous ground is often interesting.

"Pict" seems to have originated as a name for a confederation of northern tribes who fought against the Romans during the later period of the Roman occupation of Britain. The name does not appear in classical texts until the very end of the 3rd century AD, by which time it may be describing a long-established fact. And it is used to describe all of the peoples living north of the Wall – at that date, Hadrian's Wall. "Pict" is probably a real name, used locally, rather than a Roman invention (despite the attractive Latin derivation from *pictis* – painted, with the visions it conjures up of woad-decorated or tattooed warriors) for it was later adopted as a general term for people from this area, used by Scots arriving from Ireland and by Angles moving north from Northumbria. The Norse, when they arrived from Scandinavia in the late 700s or early 800s AD, clearly thought of Orkney and Shetland as Pictish. It used to be thought the Picts were a distinct and very ancient native race, but the current view is that they were not so much a race as an amalgamation of early Celtic tribes, linked by military and marriage alliances – perhaps more political than tribal.

The area which is traditionally regarded as the early heartland of the Picts, eastern Scotland north of the Central Lowlands and south of the Moray Firth, was not an area in which brochs were built. The typical Iron Age defence in these areas was the hillfort, although the coasts sported a few promontory forts not unlike those in Shetland. Indeed, it may well be that the Pictish heartland was the very area from which the threat feared by broch-builders emanated. Yet by the time the Picts emerge into the dim light of early history, these very different middle Iron Age backgrounds seem to have been merged into a single entity, uniting what older archaeologists called "the broch province" and the "fort province" – still useful descriptive terms, although unfashionable.

The usual picture presented by archaeologists and early historians is one of the steady growth of "kingdoms", which spread out to absorb ever increasing areas. On this view, Shetland would have been absorbed into Pictish territory quite late – perhaps not before 600 AD. However, there is little evidence one way or the other.

It is tempting to see this unification coming very early, perhaps even coinciding with the end of the brochs, and to see both arising as the outcomes of a general peace and disarmament imposed after the Roman incursion into the north-east which culminated in the battle of Mons Graupius in 84 AD – and let us not forget that the Romans had sent a fleet around Britain that "simultaneously discovered and conquered what are called the Orcades, islands hitherto unknown" – the phrase which Tacitus' history of the campaign places immediately before the one more familiar to Shetland readers – *dispecta est Thule* – "Thule also was descried".

More daringly still – and an idea which has yet to gain widespread acceptance in archaeo-historical circles – the actual trigger for that Roman campaign might have been a conquest or alliance between the inhabitants of the "fort province" of the north-east and the "broch province" of the far north and west.

The fall of the Brochs: Peace, Picts and Priests

The Romans, who coined the maxim *divide et impera* – divide and rule – were notoriously intolerant of alliances between tribes living on the fringes of their Empire. Our sole Roman source, Tacitus' account of the campaigns in Scotland of his father-in-law, the general Agricola, hints at just such a motivation for Agricola's push towards the Moray Firth, saying "he dreaded a general movement among the remoter tribes".

Such ideas are hard to test by archaeological methods, although obviously they would require no new broch to have been built in the north after 84 AD. The idea of the Roman pacification of the north of Scotland does provide a useful context for the very few brochs found around the Tay and upper Forth and in the Borders and the far south-west of Galloway. These would be the homes of warriors now surplus to requirements in their homeland but recruited as mercenaries on the strength of their reputation, acting as border guards between potentially hostile tribes. Parallels might be cited in later arrangements, such as the Varangian Guards of Viking origin at Constantinople, or the Gurkhas in the British Army: but that is a long and tortuous trail, and much farther away from Shetland than we want to stray.

To return to the Picts, it used to be thought that they were pre-Celtic, and spoke a non-Indo-European language, but current scholarly opinion is that the Pictish tongue was indeed a Celtic one, akin to old Welsh or very ancient Gaelic, although very few written inscriptions survive – those that do are runes of the type called "ogham", dedications carved on stone late in the Pictish period, probably after contact with Gaelic settlers from the west. But by and large, the Picts seem to have had an oral culture, reliant upon trained memory-carriers rather than written records. Their archaic Celtic language was lost – perhaps even deliberately "educated out" – when they became united with the Gaelic-speaking Scots in the 9th century AD. In Shetland, this was the time of the Viking settlement, and Shetland probably went from Pictish to Norse without an intermediate Gaelic phase. Few definite Pictish place names survive in Shetland, but it has been suggested Unst, Yell and some other island names may be of this vintage. There is only one (highly questionable) ancient Gaelic place name in the islands.

The most visible evidence for the Picts, and evidence which would justify the idea of a distinct culture even if we did not have the name "Pict" to conjure with, is the remarkable series of carved stones with elaborate symbols which occur in northern Scotland (about which more shortly), whose distribution tends to be used to define the so-called "Pictish province", although there is actually little other than geographical coincidence to link these stones, which are believed to have been created between (both dates hotly contested) about 600 AD to about 1000 AD, with the people the Romans called Picts.

Apart from the many wonderful carved stones, and some very special metalwork, there is relatively little distinctive "Pictish" archaeology, in Shetland or elsewhere. At Sandwick

Nearby, the Mail Pictish stone, showing a dog (or dolphin) headed man carrying an axe, was found in 1992 in the wall of a graveyard. It is now in the Shetland Museum, Lerwick.

of late Iron Age sites, quartz pebbles painted with abstract line and dot patterns occur, and the distribution of these so-called "Pictish pebbles" has been claimed as another cultural indicator for the elusive Picts.

Pictish symbol stones are most closely concentrated in the old counties of Angus, Perthshire, Banff, Moray, Nairn and Aberdeenshire, with strong numbers also in Fife, Inverness-shire, Ross and Cromarty and East Sutherland. They are present, though less numerous, in Caithness, Orkney, Shetland and the Inner Hebrides, and rare elsewhere. Early symbol stones are often simple slabs, boulders or outcrops which bear incised decoration in the form of animal or geometric motifs – many plausible and implausible schemes have been suggested for the meaning of these symbols – while later examples are often carved in relief upon specially prepared slabs and usually include human figures and overtly Christian symbols.

There is much debate about the meaning of symbol stones, and they have been interpreted as grave-markers, memorials, boundary markers or gathering-points. There is no doubt that they were produced locally, for they are of local stone, which tells us that wherever there is a symbol stone, there was at least one person working in the artistic idiom which today we call Pictish.

in Unst (123), a distinctive grave was excavated and dated to around 400 AD. A single skeleton lay beneath a low rectangular cairn edged with stone slabs, scattered with quartz pebbles and heaped with larger boulders. Rectangular cairns of this type also occur in Caithness. Elsewhere in northern Scotland, rectangular graves below small square or round cairns, sometimes with ditches around them, typify late Iron Age burials, so Sandwick is perhaps evidence of religious practices shared by the whole "Pictish" area. On some excavations

There are few symbol stones in Shetland, and most are of the supposedly later, overtly Christian, class. For a long time, one small scratched figure of an eagle from Islesburgh and a lost symbol stone from Cross Kirk, Esha Ness, represented the earlier class of stone, which is usually interpreted as pagan. To these was added the fine figure of a dog-headed man carrying an axe, found at Mail, Cunningsburgh, in 1992. This paucity of pre-Christian symbol stones has been used in the past to suggest that the Pictish art-style may have spread to Shetland relatively late, after the islands began to be Christianised.

However, it has already been suggested that Shetland was incorporated much earlier than this into the Pictish sphere of influence, a view which would be supported by the occurrence of the Sandwick burial (dated to around 400 AD) and the painted pebbles from the upper levels of broch sites such as Upper Scalloway. Recently, Pictish-style carvings – a small boar and a larger bear – have been recovered from excavation contexts at Old Scatness which, although apparently late, suggest that such carvings were both created and discarded before the Norse arrival. These observations may simultaneously support an early date for Shetland becoming part of the Pictish sphere of influence and require a reconsideration of the dating of the Pictish art-style generally. These recent discoveries may help to resolve the problem of the mis-match between the spread of Pictish carvings and apparent political units in the far north. But these are much larger problems, into which Shetland evidence shines a useful light, but where the applicability of the ideas suggested here needs to be considered for other areas by those who know them better.

The majority of Shetland's Pictish carved stones, however, are

Christian in content, depicting crosses, clerics and gospel symbols. They are usually associated with ancient church sites. Splendid examples have been found at St Laurence's Church, Papil (120), St Mary's, Cullingsburgh (119) and St Ninian's Isle (121). Some of these are of very high quality indeed, and as a result most have made their way to the National Museum in Edinburgh. Among the stones from St Ninian's

At Mail, Cunningsburgh, a late Iron Age building stood on this islet – was it the home of the local chief?

Early cross-marked stone from St Ninian's Isle. *Photo: Shetland Museum*

The Monks' Stone, from Papil, West Burra.
Photo: Shetland Museum

Shetland was Christianised and most districts probably had small chapels well before the date of the Norse settlement. Here, excavations are underway on an eroding chapel site at Gungstie on Noss, which has produced one corner-stone from a Pictish shrine.

Isle and from Papil are fragments of stone shrines or altars, built of slabs held together at the corners by grooved stone posts. Recently a stone corner-post (but so far no carved slabs) has come from the chapel site at Gungstie on Noss – close to an inlet called Papil Geo. One of the shrine side-slabs from Papil shows a lively scene of a group of clerics or monks, in procession, one mounted on a pony and the others on foot. One of the walking

monks carries a book-satchel, and the whole group are shown over a depiction of waves. It would require a considerable degree of perversity to interpret this sculpture as anything other than a depiction of the arrival of a community of monks from across the sea.

The evidence of the carved stones, especially the newer discoveries, tends to suggest that Shetland was already "Pictish" artistically before Christianity reached the islands. It is usually believed that Christianity was brought to Shetland by missionary clerics from Iona or one of its early daughter monasteries some time in the late 500s or early 600s, but probably not before the momentous meeting somewhere near modern Inverness around 565 AD when the high king of the Picts, Brude, was visited by Columba. The possibility remains that Christianity reached Shetland not from the Irish west but from the Pictish/ Northumbrian south. The archaeological evidence is equivocal, and much more research needs to be done to resolve this question.

All of the sites which have produced carved stones with Christian motifs are in the type of location which might be expected for a church placed to serve a local secular community. That the local communities were, by the time Christianity arrived, Pictish – whatever that means in detail – seems undeniable. The treasure from the church site at St Ninian's Isle suggests that the early church was well-endowed. That treasure, found during excavations in 1958 on the site of a succession of churches overlying an Iron Age settlement, consisted of a series of silver bowls, brooches and other items, skilfully worked with surface designs in the later Pictish mode. It is probable that these items were the property of a local cleric – perhaps the most senior

of the islands. They were probably made in northern Scotland, just possibly in Shetland itself, although they echo earlier designs from post-Roman Europe.

The diminutive scale and wide separation of early churches in the north, Shetland included, might suggest a vertically-divided society, with a wealthy ruling class who both sponsored Pictish artwork and adopted Christianity, leaving the bulk of the population to struggle on unenlightened. But this would be an unwarranted simplification. Around many of the early churches are enclosures formed by walls or earthen banks – good examples may be seen at Papil, Cullingsburgh, St Ninian's Isle and Kirkaby in Unst. Evidence from Ireland and elsewhere suggests that most public worship may have taken place in the open air, with processions around a sacred

Early churches were always near the sea. That was where the best land and the congregations were located, and longer distance travel was by water. St Ninian's Isle was the site of small Pictish and later churches. The low green mound marks the site (121).

enclosure pausing at open-air shrines and crosses: this would fit well with the carved stone evidence. The church itself would have been reserved to the ecclesiastical community, and it would have been the size of that community which dictated its dimensions, not the size of the lay congregation.

Whether or not ordinary Shetlanders of the Pictish period were as well-travelled as some were later to become, there is no doubt that the Christianising of Shetland linked the islands into a wider world than any they had previously accessed. Orders came to the church sporadically and indirectly from distant Rome, a small number of gospel books were presumably imported from scriptoria elsewhere, and the arrival of Latin allowed communication throughout Europe.

One archaeological vignette perfectly illustrates this new connectedness. Fragments of a particular type of polished stone, *porfido verde antico*, have been found at St Ninian's Isle and at Kebister – one a church site, and one a farm that later belonged to the church. This ornamental stone has its source in the eastern Mediterranean, where it was quarried and used in ancient times for decorating buildings, notably in Rome. Fragments of this stone have been found at other early Christian sites, especially at Whithorn and nearby Barhobble in Galloway. It has been suggested that some of this polished stone was brought from Rome (perhaps from the shrine of an early saint) to Whithorn, and used to build a shrine there, from which smaller chips in due course were taken out to St Ninian's followers.

It had previously been assumed that "Ninian" names in the North in Shetland (he appears as Ringan in the Gaelic West) were late in date, associated with a cult arising from a concerted campaign around the time of the Declaration of Arbroath to emphasise the distinct character of the Christian heritage of Scotland and its separateness from that of England – in short, politically correct propaganda – but the evidence of these tiny chips of marble suggests that there may, after all, have been early Ninianic missions into the far north. This would be consistent with evidence from Orkney of the "continental" character of the early church there, suggesting that the role of the Columban missions in the Christianising of the Picts may have been exaggerated in later years, when the Scots came to dominate the telling of Scotland's history and Shetland was no longer their concern. The story of the *porfido verde antico* neatly encapsulates archaeology's ability to open up huge questions which it can never resolve!

In contrast to the early church sites in the natural centres of settled farming landscapes (which in themselves imply powerful patrons, capable of giving land in such locations to the church) there is another series of sites which seem to be of early Christian date, in locations which could not be more different. Small clusters of little building foundations occur on some of the most remote, exposed and inhospitable parts of the coast. None are easy of access, and some are positively dangerous. The only convincing explanation for such sites, which occur all around the outer coasts of the British Isles, is that they are eremitical – places of hermitage to which monks retired far from human habitation, enduring lives of austere semi-starvation to send their prayers more clearly to God and to prepare their souls for their eventual passage heavenwards.

Because these sites are so awkward of access, they have been little studied, although some recent work suggests that a few were used both during the Pictish period and later, after the pagan Norse settlers had been converted in their turn.

A number of the most extreme sites have small oblong or oval foundations arranged in orderly rows, looking very like the small foundations sometimes found around ruined brochs, and probably of late Iron Age or Pictish date. At some of these sites, such as the two promontories of Kame of Isbister (116) and Birrier of West Sandwick (115), which face each other across Yell Sound, life must have been bare indeed, with nothing beyond seafowl, eggs, seaweed, shellfish, fish and perhaps the produce of a

Birrier of West Sandwick in Yell is a forbidding and exposed site, yet its seaward slopes bear traces of small structures, which may have housed eremitic monks in pre-Norse times (115).

few small plots on the hillside inland. Presumably some basic rations were supplied to the hermits by their parent religious community.

Other eremitical sites, marginally less extreme, were probably established on former fortifications – such as Ness of Garth (100). There seems to have been a Pictish tradition of giving fortified sites, presumably still high status but no longer needed as defences, to the early church. An instance is recorded in the Book of Deer, which attests to the giving of the Red Fort (probably Dundarg in Banffshire) to St Drostan. Several broch ruins in Shetland have churches on or immediately beside them, although annoyingly for extravagant theories, most are Methodist chapels and thus much, much later. However, the medieval church at Lunna clearly stands on a large broch mound, and the churchyards at Levenwick and Norwick look as if they, too, are on mounds of suitable size. It would be interesting to know what lies below the large green mound in the Tingwall graveyard on which Shetland's senior church stood in medieval times and which is now occupied by the more recent church that replaced it.

Some of the marginally more accessible coastal sites attributed to early Christian use, such as Blue Mull on Unst (114), Strandbrough on Fetlar (125) and Kirk Holm near Sand (127), have elongated bow-sided house foundations of typical Norse plan. These may indicate complexes which were farms as well as religious accommodation, self-sufficient monastic communities more in keeping with the monastic traditions of later times.

There are doubtless still more of these early ecclesiastical sites to be found, on seaward-sloping and inaccessible stacks and promontories. The key to identifying them seems to be that there is no other rational explanation for their bizarrely inconvenient siting. Not content with the exposed cliff-top location of sites like Strandbrough, there is a truly exposed cluster of foundations on the precipitous Clett, a sheer-sided rock off Fetlar (117). Sometimes placenames record old traditions of religious use, such as the forbidding Freya or Freyers (=Friars) Stack, off Foula. Some recent work has been done on the stacks off Papa Stour, but archaeology does not find it easy to study those who deliberately went without almost all material possessions and had the sea at their door to dispose of their scanty domestic refuse.

There were, of course, other purposes to which remote locations were put. In medieval and later times, Shetland had several leper-houses – these were small colonies of miserable huts out on the edge of settlements, well away from the homes of the community but close enough for donations of food to be left at agreed points along their boundary walls. The best example survives on Papa Stour. Sadly, modern science belatedly suggests that these unfortunate outcasts did not suffer from true leprosy – although this did exist in northern Europe – but were probably the victims of a skin disorder caused by excessive intake of fish and salty food. Isolation in appalling living conditions was exactly the worst treatment for them. Some of the little foundations on sea-stacks may be associated with seabird harvesting – in the Hebrides, small stone buildings are, to this day, used for a few weeks each year by men who row from the north end of the Isle of Lewis out to lonely Sula Sgeir to harvest young gannets. But Shetland traditions are strong and generally reliable, and leper houses, fishing stations and fowling sites would be – and are – remembered. Even so, some of these may have stood on older religious sites.

When all more recent uses are taken account of, there still remains a solid residue of remote sites which do not have such logical explanations and genuinely seem to represent an early Christian eremitical tradition. Visiting many of these remote sites is not possible for the casual walker – some have only been accessed in recent years by helicopter – although the walk to the nearest safe vantage point is usually worthwhile in itself, serving to reinforce the impression of these sites as located beyond the margins of everyday Shetland life, both now and in ancient times.

To return to the ordinary people, we can assume there was a reasonable-sized population to have attracted and then supported the early church. For the ordinary people of this period, Pictishness probably signified little. They probably thought of themselves as Shetlanders first and foremost, perhaps after conversion as Christian Shetlanders. They doubtless remained serenely untroubled by the questions about their "cultural identity" which so vex modern scholars.

Until the excavation of Old Scatness, Shetland was not well-supplied with dwellings for these ordinary Pictish-period Shetlanders. Only a single small house at Jarlshof and fragmentary round houses underneath the later church site at St Ninian's Isle and at Underhoull in Unst had been identified with this period. It was argued by some that, like the houses of the "ordinary people" required by certain views of the broch period, the houses of this period lay below later buildings, or as unrecognised humps and bumps in the landscape. This last explanation certainly proved to be the case at Kebister, where an assortment of scraps of middle to late Iron Age houses was found during investigation of later structures nearby. It may well be that many Pictish-period houses (and indeed houses of other periods too) were of turf or wood – and let us not forget that in a treeless Shetland, as it was by this date, a wooden house might actually have been an expression of higher social status than a stone one, requiring costly imported timber. But what the results from Old Scatness seem to be telling us is two things: firstly that houses from the very end of the Iron Age are hard to identify because, by and large, most of them look much the same as earlier houses, and secondly, that "Pictishness" began much earlier than previously assumed.

Do the Picts still remain a problem – or is it simply that we expect too much if we hope to co-ordinate archaeological, historical and art-historical lines of evidence? It seems clear that, in so far as we understand Pictish politics (which is, admittedly, not a lot), Shetland was for several

The fall of the Brochs: Peace, Picts and Priests

centuries part of Pictish territory, perhaps from as early as the end of the brochs. (Although pedants will observe that before the end of the 3rd century AD, when the word *Pict* is first mentioned in classical texts, we should refer to *proto*-Pictish instead.) Shetland was certainly within the Pictish artistic world from the time Christianity arrived around 600 AD, but almost certainly much earlier. We still are not certain how political Pictland relates to artistic Pictland, but increasingly there is evidence that there was a real coincidence. The Picts are often cited as good example of how "experts" can take a few varied attributes and use them to construct a "culture" which may have had no basis in reality – but the emerging evidence seems to be suggesting that, for once at least, the experts got it right!

One particular Pictish problem persists in the archaeological world. There has long been a feeling that something unpleasant happened in the Northern Isles towards the end of the Pictish period. On the three main excavation sites, Jarlshof, Clickimin and Old Scatness, the quality of house-building declined slowly from the high point of the brochs and wheelhouses onwards, until by the immediate pre-Viking period, buildings are little more than glorified huts. It may simply be that the need to gather together had gone, and every family had headed off into the agricultural landscape to farm independently, as they did in much earlier times, but if this is the case it is odd that we have not found any of these scattered late Iron Age houses. A similar picture prevails in Orkney, where the great broch villages at sites comparable to Old Scatness, such as Howe, Gurness and Midhowe, have visibly dwindled by this time.

This is a puzzle, because it is almost certainly exactly at this time the marvellous stones at Papil and at Cullingsburgh were being carved, which would seem to suggest a fairly stable and even comfortable population, supporting a church which in turn could support artists of great skill. The climate was experiencing a modest upturn about this time, one which would last for about 500 years, so whatever happened, it was not a repeat of the long Bronze Age decline – although there is some evidence for a succession of poor harvests in Scandinavia in the 8th century AD. So what was going on?

Of course, perhaps we are expecting too much. Looking back at the Neolithic and Bronze Age, when houses were generally scattered through the landscape rather than clustered in villages, there is a span of about 3000 years from which we have less than 100 houses – one for every 30 years. On analogy with this, if we are looking for houses in the traditional Pictish period, as opposed to the proto-Pictish period argued for above – say from 500 AD to 800 AD, then we might have expected by now to have found about 10-12 houses from this 300-year period. Adding Jarlshof to the recent discoveries at Old Scatness, that is not far from what we actually have – and this does not take into account the many small buildings set quite high into the mounds of several unexcavated brochs – so in fact there is not an acute shortage of houses from this period at all. This idea of a scarcity may arise partly because we have evidence of 80 or more brochs built over a period which may be as short or shorter than 300 years, so our expectations in terms of sites per year have been unduly raised. Add to this the fact that houses at this time do, regardless of numbers, tend to be more slightly constructed than a few centuries earlier, thus rendering their remains harder to identify in the open landscape, and the problem of their apparent scarcity disappears.

Having argued that there was a flourishing church, that Pictish (or late Iron Age) houses are not really scarce, and that there is therefore no evidence for a major population reduction in Shetland around the time the Vikings are making their first forays, it comes as something of a blow to be reminded that when the Vikings arrived they seem to have acted as if the islands were effectively uninhabited. A similar perception was carried over into the later saga accounts. There are no tales of mighty conquests in the islands. Explaining this contradiction has exercised archaeologists and historians for decades.

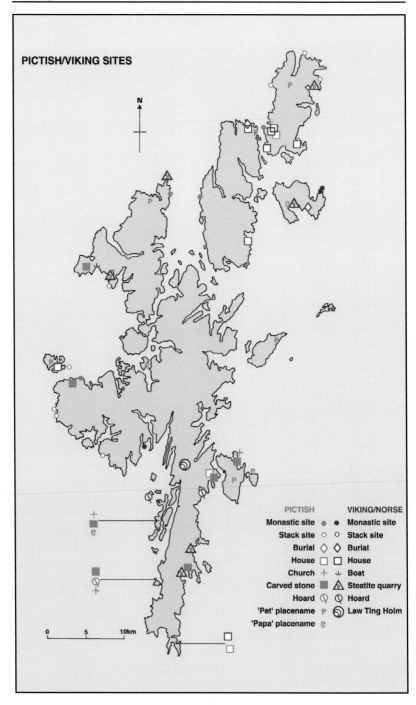

VIKINGS or Norsemen? There is a tendency to speak of "Viking" and "Norse" rather interchangeably, especially in Scotland, where most of our Vikings came from Norway rather than Denmark. It is generally accepted as correct to use "Viking" – which means "the people from the creeks" – up to about 1000 AD, the date at which the last major Viking settlements were "officially" Christianised, after which "Norse" should be used. It should, however, be noted that even the most pedantic academic will use "Viking" very loosely when trying to raise funds for a favourite project. Vikings sound more exciting! "Old Norse", or "Norn", describes the language spoken at the time of the settlement of the North Atlantic islands. Over time this has developed into Danish, Norwegian, Swedish, Faroese and Icelandic. Of these, Icelandic remains closest to the Norn tongue which would have been spoken in Shetland and of which only disjointed fragments and dialect words still survive.

Compared with their precursors in Shetland, the Picts, it is fair to say that we have a few more facts – or at least what later historians tell us are facts – about the Norse Vikings who began to settle in Shetland in numbers not long after 800 AD. We know they came predominantly from what is now western and southern Norway, that they came in considerable numbers in groups led by chieftains, and that they had little difficulty taking over the islands.

These simple facts conceal much which still remains uncertain about the exact date, the reasons and the processes behind the settlement which was to make Shetland Norse for over 600 years.

On the larger canvas, there are enough early historical sources to tell us that, by the early 800s AD, the attention of the Pictish ruling house was focussed on the south. It was shortly after this time that the Scots, who held most of western mainland Scotland north of the Clyde, and the Picts who held the eastern side and the north, came to be united under the leadership of Kenneth McAlpin, himself of part-Pictish royal descent. The struggles preceding this union of the two kingdoms to create what came to be called *Alba*, and the efforts of both sides to stave off the expansionist ambitions of the Anglian kingdom of Northumbria, left little time to consider the far north, and no forces to defend it.

Perhaps the Picts saw the Vikings as the lesser of two evils, but in any case they were apparently allowed to settle without any sustained military challenge, with the later efforts of the now unified Scottish kingdom being restricted to containing their further spread. It was not until the 12th century that the long process of reclamation of north and west Scotland was seriously begun, by a combination of military campaigns and dynastic marriages, culminating in the naval campaign and Battle of Largs in 1263 and the subsequent treaty of Perth in 1266, which formally returned all of Scotland (and added the Isle of Man, later lost) to the Scottish crown. But Orkney and Shetland were to remain under Scandinavian rule until their cession to Scotland in 1468 and 1469 respectively, in the last significant act in defining Scotland's land area as it

Point of encounter? Beneath the floor of the later chapel at St Ninian's Isle was found a hoard of silver bowls, brooches and other objects, perhaps hidden by a Pictish cleric as the Viking longships appeared around the headland (121). [Photograph taken shortly after the *Braer* oil tanker wreck in 1995. The famous beach, in the background, was breached by storm waves: nature soon repaired the damage.]

exists today. By the time they officially became part of Scotland in legal terms, the islands had already adopted Scots as a language and practiced many Scottish customs.

To return to the beginning, we can assume that, long before any settlement took place, Shetland had been inspected by Viking raiders, probably sailing both from Norway and from Denmark. The islands were probably used as a way-station on their raids down the east coast of Britain as far as northern France, and down the west coast to the Hebrides, Ireland and the Isle of Man. Although early Viking raids are customarily portrayed as targeted on the monasteries such as Lindisfarne and Iona, they also formed part of a process of sounding out the nature and military capabilities of local society and exploring the sea-routes, anchorages and land quality of the territories bordering the North Sea and the Atlantic seaboard. Whether or not this was a planned process of information-gathering, by the time the first settlers began to arrive to

stay, in areas ranging from Dublin through the Isle of Man and the Hebrides to Caithness, Orkney and Shetland, they knew exactly what they were facing in terms of landscape and had a shrewd idea of the likely level and competence of local opposition.

It is even possible there was a limited settlement in north-eastern Shetland earlier than the usually accepted dates. There is an old tradition of a distinct race, neither Picts nor Vikings, called the Finns, or Finn-Men, who are supposed to have lived in the north of Unst and the east of Fetlar, and perhaps more widely down the east coast of Shetland, leaving behind them nothing but a few place-names such as Finnister in Nesting. Were these the first Scandinavian settlers in Shetland? Finn might derive from a Pictish word akin to later Gaelic *fionn* or Welsh *wen*, both meaning fair, or white. In Ireland, later traditions speak of the Norse as *finn gall* – fair strangers.

The Norse sagas, upon which we

rely for much detail about life in these times, began to be written down in the 12th century, recording oral histories and legends of centuries gone by. They explain the settlement of Orkney (and by implication Shetland) by relating a tale of powerful chiefs falling out with the would-be king, and departing with their families, goods and gear far beyond his influence. More prosaically, climatologists tell us that the years following 800 AD saw a succession of bad harvests in Norway. Whatever the reason, a sizeable number of important men and their families and adherents made the decision to move across the North Sea and set up home in the north of what we now call Scotland. Their main objective seems to have been Orkney and the fertile plain of east Caithness, with Shetland being settled en route.

This impression, of fertile Orkney as the centre of the Norse holdings, is a theme which is frequently repeated. There was an Orkneyingasaga – the saga of the Orkneymen – which still survives. Although it seldom mentions Shetland, this does not imply a lost, parallel Shetland-specific saga, but simply that Shetland was usually seen as a poor adjunct of Orkney – perhaps echoing how things were in broch-period and Pictish times as well as how they were to become later in history. The saga writers were of the school of thought much later to be summed up by the saying that "there is properly no history, only biography". Looking back on that period, the subjects of the saga-writers' biographies, the most important and therefore most interesting people, mainly lived in

Orkney and not Shetland, and performed their most significant deeds there.

It seems to be perfectly clear that the incoming settlers were able to take over the best farmland more or less at will. Few non-Norse names survive – perhaps only some island names, Unst, Yell and Fetlar – and it always seems to have been remote or infertile places which the Norse gave names to implying they were owned by, or had been owned by, Picts – such as Pettadale, Pettifirth and Pettaster. This has led to the view that the Norse culture rapidly swamped native culture, both linguistically and in many other ways. There are few signs of any peaceful coexistence or inter-marriage, such as the late Pictish pottery and other artefacts appearing in early Norse houses, which have been tentatively identified from Orkney.

It certainly looks like a swift and effective takeover, with the local populace reduced to invisibility, and far from questioning the effectiveness of the "Norsification" of Shetland, some scholars have wondered about whether the islands were uninhabited due to some dreadful famine or plague, or whether the Picts decamped to live in areas not wanted by the new settlers. Some have even been prepared to contemplate the idea of wholesale slaughter, arguing that *petta* placenames no more mark surviving Picts in Norse times than *trow* placenames mean that trolls existed. Yet perhaps all was not blood and slaughter, for Norse placenames also commemorate the presence of Pictish Christian priests, in the *papar* names, such as Papil

Kirk Holm, near Sand, has the remains of a possible early ecclesiastical settlement at its northern end (left side in picture). Place names with "kirk" elements are widespread and usually early (127).

and Papa Stour – the big island of the priests. To modern thinking, it seems less than likely that such placenames would endure if they commemorated massacres of defenceless priests by the new settlers – but we cannot pretend to understand Norse sensibilities in these matters.

We know from the way in which the names of farms and other places are constructed (and over 99 per cent of old Shetland placenames have Old Norse derivations) and from personal names within these placenames that the bulk of the settlers came from the area around, and south of, present-day Trondheim, which not coincidentally was later to be for centuries the seat of the archbishopric including

Shetland. From the elements of placenames, it is possible to glimpse some order in the settlement process. It has been suggested that farms with names ending in *by* or *sta/ster*, such as Melby (middle farm), Norby (north farm), Bousta (principal or demesne farm) were early establishments, with *bister* farms following later, such as Symbister (south farm) and Nesbister (headland farm), then *setter* names last of all, for example Dalsetter (valley farm).

It is noticeable that, as a general rule, the earliest types of farm name do seem to be on the best farmland, but undoubtedly the process would not have been nearly as simple and straightforward as this sounds. Just as today names may have changed over time. Some settlement names would have been imported ready-made from Norway in moments of nostalgia, and other places named after landmarks, without a distinctive "farm" element in their construction – some of these may be early too, such as Hamar (steep slope) or Troswick (trolls' bay – perhaps after its prominent standing stone).

Turning to archaeological evidence, the first phase of the Norse settlement at Jarlshof is still the only excavated contender in Shetland for a Viking period house, although there are several early graves and a number of early stray finds. Recent work in Unst has identified other house sites which may be contenders for an early date, notably the site at Hamar (122) on the north side of Baltasound, which seems to have been abandoned after the primary phase of settlement: there are hopes to excavate this.

At Jarlshof (25c) the primary

The earliest house at Jarlshof, which remains the most extensive excavated Viking – Norse period settlement outside Scandinavia. Note the extreme length and the central paving (25c).

building, set in the lee of the mound containing the Iron Age and Pictish settlement – which seems to have been more or less deserted by this date – was a long hall with bowed side walls. It seems to have been undivided, except perhaps by wooden partitions. At the downslope end was the byre, a paved area with a central drain running out under the end wall. Upslope of the door, which was in the centre of one long wall, the humans lived. This space was arranged in the form of raised benches, used as living space during the day and for sleeping at night, flanking an elongated paved hearth. This impressive but simple structure was much modified over time, gaining a separate kitchen area at the top end and being extended to provide more living space, with the byre pushed further downslope. Over the generations, perhaps as new families came to the site, extra houses were built alongside. Jarlshof displays a pattern noted in the Faeroes, Iceland and Greenland, that over time houses tend to become split into separate units, with house, byre, barn and other storage all in smaller buildings linked together by passageways or door. Smaller buildings included corn-drying kilns (recently thought to be a Viking introduction, but now identified in the Pictish levels at Old Scatness) and even a possible bath-house.

It may have been only on high status sites in Shetland that specialised buildings became the norm. A note of caution is necessary here. Jarlshof is important as the first major Norse site dug outside Scandinavia, and there is always a tendency to assume that, because a site is important to archaeologists, it must also have been important at the time it was inhabited. That said, in the case of Jarlshof, it probably was genuinely important in its own time, as the ancestral residence of a local chieftain which by 1000 AD had developed into a small village, and probably even into a modest trading centre. Recent survey in Unst and studies elsewhere suggest that the elongated single-roomed house/byre survived on lower status farms as the most common type of house right into the Medieval period – as of course it survived until recently in rural areas throughout the north of Scotland.

Although Norse-period buildings had been dug at Underhoull in Unst in the 1960s, it had proved very difficult to identify many Norse period settlement sites, and the excavator of Underhoull formulated the theory (since borrowed for earlier periods) that Viking and Norse houses could not be found by landscape survey because they stood on sites which had been used continuously ever since. Since croft houses and their outbuildings have tended to get ever larger over time, especially in the 20th century, the argument was that modern crofts and farms concealed the majority of Viking and Norse farms. This rule became rather a good excuse for laziness – there was not much point in looking because we knew we were not going to find anything – and Viking or Norse houses remained rarities. Only at Sandwick in Unst and Da Biggings in Papa Stour were new Norse sites identified and excavated in the 1970s and 1980s.

In recent years, however, renewed survey has taken place, as part of a

Foundations of a Norse house at Hamar, Baltasound (122). One of the least disturbed of many such sites recently recognised in Unst.

large project involving input from Scandinavian experts as well as British. This has resulted in the discovery of around 30 Norse house sites in Unst. Most appear as foundations of solidly built, near-rectangular structures, which often lie below the ruins of later crofts, themselves abandoned. These house

Norse house at Sandwick, Unst, during excavation. The elongated rectangular plan of the house is distinctive.

foundations are aligned up and down the slope, and frequently there is a small hollow outside the downslope end, marking the point where the drainage from the byre was gathered for re-use as manure. In some cases, traces remains of large yards around these houses, bringing to mind the "home fields" so often mentioned in the Norse sagas. Trial excavations on several of the Unst houses have confirmed the presence in their interiors of typical side benches, and larger digs on two have confirmed their Norse date and established several phases of use and modification, although so far no evidence has come for the very earliest period of settlement, the "true" Viking period.

It must be admitted, to the shame of the archaeological profession, that many of the Unst house sites were not new discoveries at all, having been identified by a local enthusiast, Peter Moar, in the 1960s and 1970s. However, because it was almost an article of faith that Viking or Norse houses were rare, no British professional archaeologist at that time was prepared to believe a claim, especially one made by an amateur, that Unst could possibly have so many visible examples. One is forcibly reminded of the reluctance of an earlier generation of "experts" to believe that Shetland could possibly have so many upstanding prehistoric houses.

Doubtless survey elsewhere in Shetland will turn up more such houses, now that archaeologists know what they are looking for, although the general idea of continuity of use of sites has not been abandoned – after all, the Unst sites are all either isolated or lie below small, deserted crofts, suggesting that we are still only seeing the less successful Norse farms. For example, suspected Norse period house remains were identified in the early 1990s during building work at a crofthouse in Fetlar. These were partially excavated in 2002 and produced well-made artefacts of steatite, including many loom-weights and a huge, intact, bowl.

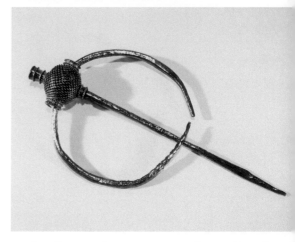

Typical domestic artefacts from the Viking and Norse periods include fragments of bone combs, glass beads (typically blue) and objects made of steatite. These things often turn up in eroding sand-dunes, emphasising the frequency with which Norse houses were sited near to the shore. Excavations at Jarlshof and other sites have produced a much greater range of domestic objects. Stone vessels, usually of steatite, are very frequent, with pottery less so. A stone speciality is a flat, plate-like vessel, which seems to have been for baking bread or oatcakes – oats having reached Shetland (and Scandinavia) some time in the Iron Age. Stone was also used for net-sinkers, whetstones and querns to grind corn. Bone artefacts such as pins, combs and handles for metal tools are also common, some beautifully carved, and glass beads are not rare, suggesting life was by no means at a basic subsistence level. Perhaps the most charming finds have been simple bone and stone toys, including a number of miniature rotary querns. Metal objects were widely used, although often these iron and bronze items have corroded away, leaving just their bone handles. Silver was used throughout the Viking world, both

as jewellery and as a means of exchange. There have been chance discoveries of some beautiful silver objects, notably the Oxna and Gulberwick brooches. It was during this period that coinage first appeared in Shetland, although it

Norse silver brooch from Gulberwick, south of Lerwick. *Photo: Shetland Museum*

Steatite outcrops on the Hillswick cliffs have been worked, despite their precarious location.

In this excavated section of the great steatite outcrop on the hillside at Catpund, Cunningsburgh, the marks left by the removal of bowl-shapes can be clearly seen (129).

An oval, boat-shaped stone setting at Breakon, North Yell may mark a Viking grave (32a).

seems to have remained scarce into medieval times, with most trade continuing to take place largely by barter.

Shetland offered one huge economic asset which Orkney did not, and that was its extensive deposits of steatite; primarily at Cunningsburgh (129) but also at other locations such as Hillswick and Houbie. Known from prehistoric times, these outcrops would have been immediately familiar to the incoming Vikings, who had extensive deposits of steatite in their home country. The abundance of steatite on Viking and Norse period sites in Norway and in Shetland suggest that, when available, it was preferred to pottery, and of course it could be used for much more than just cooking vessels and containers. Steatite was, however, very heavy, and it must have been a great bonus to the settlers to discover that they would not need to ship supplies across from Norway. It is likely, although its complex geology has so far defeated chemical proof, that much of the steatite which occurs in Viking and Norse sites in Scotland and Ireland is of Shetland, rather than Norwegian origin. Control of such a resource must have been an important consideration, in prehistoric times as well as in Norse times, and it may be more than coincidental that the name given to the area with the main workings was Cunningsburgh – the king's fort.

Apart from the economic aspects of the Viking/Norse period, such as steatite workings, the burgeoning number of settlement sites and some striking stray finds, Shetland can also boast evidence of religious practices. Burials have been found which seem

to be of the pagan Viking period, with characteristic domed "tortoise" brooches – cloak fasteners often buried as part of the costume of the deceased – which are often all that survives in graves. A few boat-shaped settings of large stones may mark graves similar to those from the Isle of Man and elsewhere in the Norse Atlantic, for example at Breakon in Yell (33b). Elongated oval mounds are known, for example near to the medieval church (and broch) site at Lunna. These mounds may well be graves of Viking date, but hopes that they may all conceal actual wooden boats buried with the deceased seem optimistic. Most boat burials so far found tend to be marked on the surface, if they are marked at all, only by upright stones. However, the presence of iron boat rivets of Viking type in an elongated mound at Aith in Fetlar (126), excavated unscientifically some years ago, holds out hope of finding something in Shetland to

match the fine burial discovered a few years ago on Sanday, in the north of Orkney – here too, the timbers of the boat had gone, leaving only the pattern of rivets.

In pagan Viking times, it was normal to bury the dead in full costume – probably their very best outfit – with weapons for men and valuable household items and jewellery for women, although this sexual stereotyping is not total, and women's graves containing weapons have been found. After the arrival of Christianity in the Norse world, elaborate burials with grave-goods cease, making it much harder to ascribe dates to graves. However, during excavations at Kebister, near Lerwick (118), two simple graves were found. These were aligned E-W, which is usually a sign of Christian graves, and contained simple pine coffins which allowed radiocarbon dating to the later 10th century AD.

When was Viking Shetland converted to Christianity? The sagas

Kebister, at the northern end of the limestone-rich Tingwall valley, under excavation in 1985. This multi-period site yielded evidence for an early wooden building which may have been a chapel, and artefacts suggesting distant Christian connections. In later centuries it saw the building of a substantial tithe barn for Shetland's archdeacon (118).

suggest that the conversion took place at a single point in time, in 995 AD when Olaf Tryggvesson mounted a campaign to force all the Norse colonies to convert. But if such a royal intervention happened at all, it was probably more of an official or symbolic conversion – in effect making Christianity the "established" religion. All the evidence from Shetland and elsewhere is that the effective conversion had taken place earlier. Even in Iceland, the most traditional of the Viking territories, there were a substantial number of Christian families by the date of the official conversion in 1000 AD. Interestingly, personal names in one of the chief Icelandic families supporting Christianisation hint at links with Shetland.

It has already been mentioned that the Vikings, when they arrived in Pictish, Christian, Shetland gave names with the element papa or papar – meaning priest – to places which either had ecclesiastical communities when they arrived, or were regarded as church property. Similar names occur widely in Orkney and in the Hebrides as well. It seems as if the Vikings were

prepared to tolerate the continuation of Christianity, and went so far as according it a degree of legitimacy by recognising it in placenames – which does not sit very well with those who argue for takeover with fire and the sword.

The pagan Viking religion was essentially a personal, family, set of beliefs. The names of the Gods were not used as war-cries, nor was it an evangelical religion. One can picture the newly-arrived Viking shaking his head in bewilderment over the "crazy Christians" perched like puffins on their promontories and rock stacks. Their reaction to the churches which sat in the middle of the best farmland and the most prosperous communities, to which in general the *papar* names were given, may have been less tolerant, but even there we have hints of a rapidly acquired accommodation. The St Ninian's Isle treasure may well have been hidden by its Pictish owner because he feared its loss in a Viking raid, but did he perhaps bury it within the church because churches themselves, as opposed to their valuables, were less likely to be destroyed than secular buildings? That is not a question we are ever likely to answer conclusively.

What we do see, is that at a date not too long after the Viking settlement, is the erection on some of the older Christian sites of typical "Norse" elongated rectangular buildings. Sites such as Strandburgh (125) and Kirk Holm (127) are the best examples. One wonders how many years it was before the peaceful Pictish Christian priests and monks began to make their first Viking converts, perhaps aided by Christian Pictish women married,

The Law Ting Holm in Tingwall Loch hosted meetings of Shetland's Norse period thing, or parliament (128).

willingly or not, into the families of Viking newcomers or serving as nursemaids to Viking children.

Unlike Orkney, Shetland lacks conclusive evidence for churches of the late Viking or early Norse date, although a small wooden rectangular building found at Kebister (118) has the correct dimensions and is close to the two oriented Christian graves already mentioned. Tradition points to sites such as Papil (120) and St Ninian's Isle (121) as centres of the early Norse church, just as they were for the Pictish church, but the one site which seems to emerge early as pre-eminent, and remains so until the Reformation, is Tingwall, set in the heart of its fertile limestone valley. Tingwall means parliament field, or valley, and it was here in Norse times that the chief men of Shetland met to decide important matters of law. The *thingstead*, or meeting site, can still be seen on a little island in the loch, with a causeway leading to the shore (128). On the rise to the north, directly in line with the causeway, is Tingwall church. The modern church stands over the ruins of a late medieval church, which doubtless lies over still earlier remains. Is the church here because of the *thing* site, or was the *thing* here because of the church? As well as the high *thing* – what in Icelandic parlance would be the Althing – there were also district *things* which dealt with more routine business, and it is surely no accident that many of the medieval parishes of Shetland more or less coincided with the districts covered by these, for example Delting, Aithsting, Sandsting and Nesting.

With regard to the organisation of

Overlooking the Law Ting Holm, Tingwall's church stands on an ancient site – the remains of the late medieval church survive as burial vaults.

the early church, Shetland continued, throughout the Norse period, to be rather in the shadow of Orkney. When in due course Orkney became a bishopric, Shetland was attached to it more or less automatically. The church never acquired great estates in Shetland as it did in Orkney, presumably because the leading churchmen were Orkney-based, mingled there with the Earls and chief men, and made it their business to acquire the most fertile land on offer. The very earliest surviving document originating in Shetland – from 1299 – hints at a pattern of absentee landlordism which may be typical. It was drawn up by the steward of Duke Hakon's farm on Papa Stour – clearly an important official, but one whose principal does not expect to visit him very often and had given him considerable executive authority. Recent excavations at Da Biggings on Papa Stour have almost certainly identified the remains of the high-status farm in question, represented by an elaborate wooden building set within a soil stone-built outer wall.

Modern Shetlanders display an extreme attachment to their "Viking roots", particularly in preference to

Most rural Shetland houses were thatched until the mid 20th century, retaining many characteristics of their Norse forebears. This is the Shetland Croft House Museum, Southvoe, Dunrossness.

Detail of thatching: note the twisted straw ropes holding the anchor stones.

any suggestion of Scottishness. This is despite the fact that, in a generation's time, Shetland will have been Scottish for longer than it was Norse. Indeed, given the fact that it was very "Scottified" in many ways before 1469, this is arguably true already. This emotional predisposition to be Vikings can require tactful presentation from students of anthropology, human biology or history, for the evidence available from anatomical studies, from genetics such as blood-types and new DNA studies, and from historical documents all suggest a very mixed ancestry, with Norse elements by no means preponderant.

But Shetlanders can, at least, claim an unchallenged Norse pedigree for their homes: in shape, layout and location, the dwellings of rural folk changed only in minor detail from the arrival of the Vikings to the mid 20th century.

Another undoubted Norse legacy is the so-called "Norse mill" or "click mill". These little mills continued to be built until the 19th century, and a few remained in use until the mid 20th century. Their characteristic ruins, occasionally re-thatched and refurbished, dot the banks of small streams throughout Shetland. A small horizontal paddle-wheel set under the mill-house directly drives the upper stone of what is little more than an enlarged rotary quern, of the type which, in hand-driven form, had arrived around the same time as the brochs. It was suggested a few years ago that these mills might be a later introduction, but the excavation of one in a firmly dated Norse-context at Orphir in Orkney proved their pedigree satisfactorily.

Even if they did not invent it, the Vikings may safely be credited with picking up the click-mill idea and spreading it, either from the Mediterranean (where it goes back to Roman times) or from Ireland (where a very similar mill has turned up recently in excavations with dates before the arrival of the Vikings there). Of course, none of the many mills in the Shetland landscape today are 1000 years old, all having been rebuilt many times over the centuries, so that few of the extant examples are much more than a century old. But the type is Norse, once again reminding us of the considerable continuity from the 9th to 19th centuries. The Viking settlement can in many ways be regarded as the beginning of modern Shetland rather than the end of ancient Shetland.

The topic of "Norse" mills and the persistence of local tradition is one that draws us towards our conclusion. Surveys of the remains left behind by early Shetlanders repeatedly throw up instances of dating by "local tradition" which seem to work very well. Shetlanders have for a long time habitually recognised various "folk" who are associated with different types of ruin. The "trows" (trolls) or "peerie (little) folk" are almost exclusively associated with pre-Iron Age sites, for example the houses and fields at Trolligarts (14) or the burnt mound at Trowie Loch in Nesting. Next come the "Picts", who according to tradition built the brochs, forts, some unexcavated green mounds

and the souterrains. Perhaps not the Pict that the art-historian recognises, but perhaps not so far away after all, as has been argued in the preceding chapter. The mysterious "Finn-Men" have no archaeology of their own (so far), only the attributions of places like the Funzie Girt dyke in Fetlar – which archaeologists would prefer to see dating from "trowie" times. When we come to the Vikings, or Norsemen, we find that only sites which are obviously more recent than brochs or cairns tend to be labelled with their name, and it has to be said the term is used fairly indiscriminately, for oldish-but-not-very-old sites. Last of all, and outwith the scope of this volume, are sites attributed to the "Dutchmen", the

A "Norse" mill, reconstructed in working order, at Shetland Croft House Museum. The form of these mills is a Norse legacy, though few actual ruins visible today are older than the 19th century.

Ruined mills, sluices and lades are widespread. Their small scale allowed them to work efficiently with the water supply available from Shetland's streams. This example is at Dutch Loch on Papa Stour.

Boats in Shetland have distinctive lines and build, probably due more to recent contacts with Scandinavia than to direct Viking legacy. Out Skerries.

Hanseatic traders and Low Countries fishermen who receive the credit for various mounds and ruined buildings near to the shore, for example the "Hollanders knowes" or the "Dutchmen's graves".

It has been suggested by sceptics that this "traditional" attribution and naming is something which has arisen since Victorian times, but at least for the *trow* names this can be shown not to be the case, for they are much older and were being used to form Norse placenames – as for example Troswick – many centuries before the time of the first recorded antiquarians.

In any case, as the re-discovery of the Norse houses of Unst has shown, there is a remarkable store of knowledge embedded in Shetland lore. One of the most positive developments of the last two

decades has been the increase in collaboration and dialogue between visiting archaeologists and local people. In Shetland, more than most places, geography, prehistory, history and tradition are woven together in a way which can allow valid inferences about the past, and it is immensely heartening to see these strands being drawn ever more closely together in each succeeding year's research programmes. Gone, hopefully forever, are the days when an archaeological team arrived, dug a site for no obvious reason and then disappeared "south" again, with no-one in Shetland – sometimes not even the Museum – being any the wiser about their findings until years later, and no opportunity for the local inhabitants to point out the *really* interesting site just over the hill. Nowadays archaeologists tend to accept that there can be no-one better placed to understand prehistoric and early historic life than a crofter living in a house on a thousand-year-old site and farming and fishing in a style which, mechanisation apart, may have changed little in its essentials for even longer.

Likewise, those of us who visit Shetland mainly in the summer months now recognise that we will always be at a disadvantage compared with those who live there all year long, especially when it comes to thinking about landscape matters such as the location of brochs or the feasibility of Pictish invasions. The Up-Helly-A "Viking" celebrations may be a Victorian fantasy and not a Viking tradition, but all archaeologists should be required to attend, if only so they come to appreciate what Shetland is like in the short, dark, windy days of midwinter, as well as the long gentle days of the summer digging season.

So, as those who are reading this guide visit the many sites discussed and described here: remember that what you are looking at are the vestiges of real people, individuals whose works have been preserved from oblivion by the hand of fate. Look around at the green fields and remember that the soil of each fertile acre was won painstakingly from barren moorland. The past is very close to the surface in Shetland, and in Shetlanders. As a local antiquarian put it many years ago, "in short, there must have taken place the same constant warfare against cold and hunger that has ever gone on in Shetland".

Endpiece: sunset at Wood Wick in Unst.

Gazetteer

THIS is a selective list including the best examples of all periods and types. It is not comprehensive: some fine sites are not listed here, mainly because they are hard to locate or difficult of access. A few are listed here not so much for what remains to be seen on site, but because they enjoy splendid settings – this is made clear in individual entries. The best-preserved sites of each category are marked with an asterisk, and would serve for the visitor pressed for time to gain a good general impression of what Shetland has to offer.

Entries are arranged by broad period. Within each period they are arranged geographically: Unst, Yell, Fetlar, Whalsay, Mainland (arranged N, E, W then S), Fair Isle. Other islands are dealt with alongside the adjacent part of Mainland. The Ordnance Survey 1:50 000 sheet number (Shetland is covered by sheets 1 to 4) is given for each site, followed by its two-letter, six-figure grid reference – accurate to within about 50m, which is close enough to see each site in normal conditions. It is best to obtain and use map and compass and not to rely solely on the directions given here, although these have been checked over several editions. Most sites are marked individually on the OS maps: usually appearing as a small symbol with a generic name such as "cairn" or "broch – rems of". The few that do not appear are marked NOM (not on map) in the gazetteer.

Directions are given to each site from the public road, by either the shortest or the least complicated route. Walking distances given here are one way only, and in most cases involve crossing one or more fences or walls, which do not always have conveniently-sited gates.

Only two sites currently have admission charges and limited visiting hours: Jarlshof (Gazetteer entry 25) and Old Scatness (108). Inclusion here does not imply right of access. Most sites are on open moorland or fenced grazing land and freely accessible to any visitor who takes care not to disturb livestock or to damage walls and fences, secures gates or leaves them open as found, and generally behaves sensibly. If in doubt: ask locally. Car-drivers should park considerately, not blocking gates, passing places or turning areas. Dogs, however well-trained, should be kept on the leash at all times when on farm or croft land, and always well away from livestock. If it is necessary (it seldom is) to cross a field under crop, keep to the field edges – and please remember that grass is a crop, too, and a very important one in Shetland. Some sites are a considerable distance from roads and in uninhabited country with few casual passers-by. Be well-clothed and if you are venturing any distance from the road, take a map and compass and be able to use them: Shetland's weather changes swiftly, and thick fog is a local speciality, especially in summer.

These sites represent the legacy of generations who have left no other record of their passing, and are precious fragments of our heritage. Do not scramble over crumbling walls, dig for any reason or try your hand at rebuilding. Leave things as you find them, so that future generations may enjoy the pleasure of searching out these traces of their earliest ancestry for themselves. On a more serious note: almost all of the sites listed are protected by law as scheduled ancient monuments, and it is a criminal offence to disturb them or to use a metal detector on them or close by.

Good visiting. Once you have exhausted this list, many other archaeological sites marked on the Ordnance Survey 1:50000 maps are worth a look, and larger-scale maps often have extra sites – those for Unst, Papa Stour, West Mainland and Fair Isle are particularly rich in this respect. Shetland's archaeology is by no means completely surveyed and recorded, so there is always a chance of discovering new sites. If you think you have discovered an artefact or an unrecorded site, you should inform the correct organisation: see local contacts at the end of this book.

Neolithic/Bronze Age - settlement

1 *Funzie Girt, Fetlar, boundary dyke   1 HU617931 – HU626945
A long stretch of remarkably massive tumbled drystone walling, running across the shoulder of the hill. This is probably the finest prehistoric boundary dyke in Shetland. (Park at airstrip, then a 2km walk north, past Hjaltadans (36), over the saddle between Stackaberg and Vord Hill. The dyke runs from the saddle N, then NW, around the side of the hill, ending near the impressive cliffs at East Neep.) Important note: site lies in a Special Protection Area, which is very important for breeding birds. Between 1 March and 11 August, do not visit before contacting Fetlar-based RSPB Warden on 01957 733

246. Access is usually possible, but Warden has final decision.

2 *Benie Hoose, Whalsay, house
2 HU586653
This fine example of a cloverleaf plan house, close to a second (3), was excavated by Charles Calder, the excavator at Stanydale (18). Despite the presence of a number of cairns of possible heel-shaped plan in the vicinity, there is no reason to suppose that either the Benie Hoose or Yoxie was anything other than a typical farmhouse. (Park near Isbister and walk 1km NE, skirting above the shore. In dry weather the approach over the hill from the N, parking near Muckle Breck, is a pleasant alternative walk of similar length.)

3 *Stones of Yoxie, Whalsay, house   2 HU587653
Just downslope from the Benie Hoose (2), this too is an excavated example of a simple prehistoric house. The "forecourt" of the "temple", as interpreted by the excavator, is probably no more than a large porch or windbreak protecting the entrance. (Access as for Benie Hoose.)

4 Loch of Sandwick, Whalsay, houses & fields   2 HU536617
Remains of at least four prehistoric houses of varied plan, together with two burnt mounds and several stretches of field walling occupy an extensive area on the northern shore of Sand Wick. (400m to 600m W from the road, steeply down hill between the Sandwick crofts – numerous fences make this an awkward site to access.)

Gazetteer

5 Beorgs of Uyea, North Roe, stone axe quarry 2 HU327900

A large outcrop of felsite, quarried to produce a hollow, which has been roofed over. The felsite was used for the production of polished stone knives and axes, and the litter from the roughing-out of these tools lies all around the quarry pit. It includes semi-finished rough-outs abandoned before final polishing began. This is the most easily found of a number of working floors spread across the nearby slopes, where this favoured rock-type outcrops in many places. (A good track runs W from North Roe School for 3km, until it swings NE. From this point, the route to the site is along the S shore of the Mill Loch for just under 1km. Head for a tall, modern cairn on the skyline: the site is reached just before this. A rough track through unfrequented moorland to a remote site.)

6 Black Water, Eshaness, house 3 HU229786

A ruinous oval house of rather small dimensions. (Immediately beside the N edge of the B9078 road, 300m beyond the turnoff for Leascole.)

7 Grevasand, Hillswick, house 3 HU274762

An oval house, with many traces of field boundaries and small cairns nearby. (On a dip in the ridge on the W side of Ness of Hillswick peninsula, just under 1km SW of the road end near Findlins in Hillswick village. If visiting this site, it is worth taking in Niddister burnt mound (72) and also looking (with care) at the cliffs on the W side of the peninsula, which have steatite outcrops.)

8 Punds Water, Mangaster, house and walls 3 HU323714

A massively built house, with an associated field system apparently bounded by a stout wall, which closes the neck of a promontory just beyond the house. (750m NW, mainly on steep grass, from parking place on road just E of Mangaster, over a small hill, to the chambered cairn (47), then a further 500m over heathery ground around the S shore of Punds Water.)

9 *Bays Water, Mavis Grind, houses & fields 3 HU335675

A well-preserved field system, incorporating four houses, one of which, an oval 11m by 9, is apparently of a similar plan to the main house at Gruting School (19). There are many clearance cairns, and a number of "rude stone implements", mainly stone plough tips, have been found in this area. (At the N end of Bays Water. Most easily reached from the public road just NW of Busta House, then 1km NW over a mainly grassy hill, finally dropping down towards the site.)

10 Lunning, Lunnasting, house 3 HU510671

A well-preserved prehistoric house, standing up to 1m high. The structure is 10m in diameter, with a thick wall surrounding an interior that has traces of four alcoves. The entrance was on the south side, where there is an annexe, or a small yard. To the NE is a small field or yard, and to the E field walling is visible. (150m S of the trig point on Lunning Head, a 300m walk NE from the public road end at Lunning.)

11 *Newing, South Nesting, houses & fields

3 HU467559 – HU477567 (NOM)

A remarkable series of prehistoric houses and enclosures, together with clearance cairns and walls, beside the North Nesting road. A small house in a field system lies 200m W of the deserted croft at South Newing (HU467558), and another immediately E of the road 100m E of the croft (HU470559), has a windbreak outside its entrance. 500m along the road, beyond North Newing and at the foot of the road embankment, is a third example (HU474565). This is roughly circular, with numerous field walls nearby. 170m further on, and near the E side of the road, is an oval house 8m by 7, with its entrance on the SE and an enclosure attached to its SW side. The final example (HU477567) immediately beside the road on the E, lies 120m beyond, and is 8m by 6, again with an entrance on the SE side. (Ranged along the B9075 road running N from the Skellister junction, none of the houses is far from the road.)

12 Finnister, houses and fields

3 HU462517 (NOM)

Two simple oval houses lie on the hillside, near to a perennial spring, with a splendid view across the Isles of Gletness. (Simplest route is to park beside the road at about HU466523 and head SW, keeping just above the deserted croft and walled/fenced area around it, to reach the houses on the upper side of a S-facing dip just beyond. The houses lie a little higher than the level of the croft, and can be hard to spot.)

13 Longa Ness, Noonsbrough, houses

3 HU288579 (NOM)

Two prehistoric houses lie in a low valley between Longa Ness and North Ward of Noonsbrough, with a series of field walls and clearance cairns around them. One of the houses lies directly below a sheep shelter, the second being about 100m to the E. A ruined cairn lies on a hillside ledge overlooking the settlement area from the E. (From road end at Noonsbrough, walk along track past farm and then head NW over hilltop and steeply down to the site, about 1km.)

14 Trolligarts, Sandness Road, houses & fields

3 HU245524 (NOM - site well S of placename on the 1:50000 map)

Two oval houses (at least) and a complex scatter of field walls and clearance cairns lie around and below a group of later croft buildings, sheep pens and cabbage patches. Two chambered cairns lie nearby. This site has never been properly surveyed, and is potentially as extensive and interesting as any in West Mainland Shetland. (250m NE of the A971 Sandness road, park near the point where a small stream flows into W end of Loch Flatpunds.)

15 *Scord of Brouster, Bridge of Walls, houses, cairns & fields

3 HU255516

16 Pinhoulland, Bridge of Walls, houses, cairns & fields

3 HU259497

17 Loch of Grunnavoe, Bridge of Walls, houses

3 HU258494

These locations are the nuclei of an extensive belt of early agricultural settlement remains running down the W side of the Voe of Browland. Brouster, excavated in the late 1970s, has four houses, a possible square, kerbed, burial cairn, a system of interlinked field walls and over 100 clearance cairns. The main house at Brouster has massive upright stones dividing the side alcoves, and dates to before 2000 BC, when it replaced an earlier wooden structure. Some of the cairns, which look small, have sub-peat basal diameters of over 2m. There is good evidence from this site that soils in the area were much richer during the early settlement phase. Published excavation report on Scord of Brouster. Pinhoulland has as many as seven houses, a few short traces of walls and many cairns. Grunnavoe has three houses and many cairns. Between these are numerous field-clearance cairns and stretches of walling, often partly submerged by the peat. Associated with this assemblage are a number of larger cairns, some of them chambered (see 58). (Brouster is reached from the Sandness road about 250m W of the Bridge of Walls junction, from which it is a 200m walk to the N; Pinhoulland from the Walls road 500m SW of the same junction, then walking SSE for 600m; Grunnavoe most easily from the Walls to Whiteness minor road, walking 1km NE to, and then along, the N shore of Loch of Grunnavoe, alternatively by extending the walk from Pinhoulland S for a further 600m.)

18   *Stanydale, "temple" & houses   3 HU285502
The best known, although by no means the most extensive, of the prehistoric settlement areas in West Mainland Shetland, Stanydale is remarkable for the main structure, which is a double-sized version of the oval transepted house. Three rather ruined oval houses of normal size lie near to the main building, while a fourth, which is in a clearer state, lies on the approach track. Numerous fragments of walling lie around the area, with a large number of grass-grown clearance cairns. A setting of upright stones curves round the south side of the main building. A number of burial cairns lie on hilltops overlooking the site from N and S. The main building has two post-holes in the centre, and may have been roofed, a formidable undertaking   in   wood-scarce Shetland. Its entrance is from the centre of a curved façade like that of the heel-shaped cairns and the size and plan of the structure led the excavator to suggest that the building was a temple. It must certainly have been an edifice of some importance, and presumably some sort of gathering place, whether religious or secular. The well-preserved house nearby, which has been excavated, shows a variant on the usual plan, with a main oval chamber from which a small circular compartment runs off at the inner end. The entrance has been provided with a porch, or windbreak, curving around the doorway, which could otherwise have been exposed to the SW. Pottery from this house and the "temple" suggests a long period of use, from the late Neolithic right through the Bronze Age. Guardianship monument, always open. See also Historic Scotland guidebook. (Signposted from

roadside, route marked by posts for 800m across grassy moorland. Park at signpost beside Gruting road 1km S of the junction for Stanydale farm. Do not take the road to Stanydale farm.)

19 Gruting School, houses
3 HU282499

A large oval house lying north of the head of Gruting Voe is the best-preserved member of a group of three houses. The second has been bisected by the road, and lies lower down the hill, while the third lies below a small garage beside the road. (The first house is 20m N of the road, just above the access to the former Gruting School, now a private home.)

20 Ness of Gruting, houses & fields
3 HU276483 - HU283482

Two groups of remains lie close together. Two houses and a burnt mound lie on the SW ridge of the hill. Further to the E is a single house. Both groups lie within enclosures, and the hillside is divided up into a series of small fields, some of which appear to be terraced into the slope. (The easiest approach is along the ridge from the highest point on the road between Seli Voe and Scutta Voe for approximately 1km. The site lies halfway down the slope to the shore and is fairly easy to spot as the descent begins to steepen.)

21 *Clickimin, Lerwick, house
4 HU464408

A small, heavily rebuilt, oval house of cloverleaf plan represents the first phase of a long use of the site, and may have had other, less substantial, buildings around it. (See below for Iron Age elements.) Guardianship

monument, no charge. See also Historic Scotland guidebook. (Signposted to right of the A970 road heading S through the suburbs of Lerwick, not far beyond a roundabout.)

22 Punds Geo, Uppersound, house
4 HU458392

A ruined house, 10m by 7, lies on a small terrace. The entrance seems to be on the W side. Another, more ruined structure, lies 100m to the N, and may also be a house. (Park near school and walk down towards head of bay, round to W side and then S along a path through heathery ground on the W side of the bay. About 1km from the head of the bay.)

23 Ux Ness, West Burra, house & field
4 HU383357 (NOM)

A small, oval house with large blocks forming the partitions between the internal alcoves. A boundary wall encloses the house and a number of clearance cairns. (Immediately beyond the edge of the bridge from Trondra to West Burra, on the right and just above the road.)

24 Dalsetter, Boddam, houses & fields
4 HU403157

Three oval houses lie within a fragmentary enclosure wall built of large blocks. Within the main enclosure are traces of slighter walls, and a number of clearance cairns testify to early agriculture. The houses are of medium size, from 10m to 12 in overall length. (Close to E side of road from Boddam to Troswick, on S-facing slope to N of modern houses and visible from the road. Field gate from the road at the N end of the site.)

25 *Jarlshof, Sumburgh, houses
4 HU398096

The earliest remains visible at this, the most complex excavated site in Shetland, comprise a cluster of smallish oval houses, which show the characteristic "clover-leaf" internal plan. These were replaced towards the end of the Bronze Age by a group of roughly circular houses, of similar size. A number of querns, used for grinding grain, have been left in situ, and more artefacts can be seen in the visitor centre. (See below for Iron Age and later remains.) Guardianship monument, visitor centre open during summer only, admission charge. Contact 01950 460112 (out-of-season, 01856 841815). See also Historic Scotland guidebook. (Signposted, parking at Sumburgh Hotel, then 200m surfaced path to site.)

Neolithic/Bronze Age –
ritual and funerary

26 Muckle Heog, Unst, cairns
1 HP630108, HP631107

On the summit of the hill are the remains of a large cairn that was excavated in the 19th century and produced bones and steatite pottery. Not far to the NW is a heel-shaped cairn with traces of the façade showing, and the remains of two cists, but no trace of a chamber. (Summit of hill, 700m WNW from entrance to Hagdale. A stiff climb.)

27 Rounds of Tivla, Unst, cremation cemetery 1 HP616107

Downhill from a group of three round cairns, one containing a cist, lies this group of three circular earthworks. Only one retains its earlier recorded form, and this consists of three low concentric banks, with two shallow ditches between, surrounding a central stony spread some 9m in diameter. The ruined sites nearby were apparently of similar character. This may be a Bronze Age burial monument of a type related to the enclosed cremation cemeteries of more southern parts. (Near the top of Crussa Field, 1km NE from Gue, Baltasound. A fair weather alternative is to continue 1.5km W, over Nikka Vord, after visiting Muckle Heog (26).)

28 Hill of Caldback, Unst, chambered cairn
1 HP607067, HP604066 (NOM)

Two heel-shaped cairns stand on this hill. The one on the summit (shown on map) is badly dilapidated, but measures about 16m across, with a façade on the eastern side. There are no clear signs of cist or chamber. The lower cairn, at the foot of the slope on the west side of the hill (NOM), is better preserved, and of similar dimensions. Two large upright blocks frame the façade, and the cairn is unusual in having three cists, but no entrance passage and chamber. This is the only definite example of the combination of a heel-shaped cairn with cists, rather than with a burial chamber and passage. (The hill is W of the highest point on the A968 Baltasound-Uyeasound road.)

29 Watlee, Unst, chambered cairn
1 HP596051

A smaller cairn, 10m in diameter, with vague traces of a central chamber. A small oval foundation on the north side is later. (The cairn lies immediately W of the main A968 road, overlooking Loch of Watlee.)

30 *Bordastubble, Burragarth, Unst, stone 1 HP578034
Possibly the most massive of the Shetland standing stones, this example is of gneiss, stands 3.8m high and is up to 2.7m thick. Traces of packing stones can be seen at the foot of the stone, but it is not certain that these are original rather than a later attempt to prop up the block, which leans towards the southwest. (A short distance N of the road to Lund, 350m beyond the point where it branches off the Westing road.)

31 Clivocast, Unst, standing stones 1 HP604005, HP606007
A slender stone, 3m tall but only 0.9m wide at the base, stands on the slopes above Uyea Sound. A second, squatter, monolith stands down-slope. A possible Viking grave was found many years ago near the latter stone. (S of the road to Muness, on the hillside overlooking Uyea.)

32 Breakon, Yell, cairns and other remains 1 HP528053
A rather ruinous oval house is one of the features of this sand-dune area, which also has several substantial but rather featureless cairns and enclosures, as well as a possible Viking grave (see below). (Follow track from Breakon Farm 350m down to shore, heading for sandy bay.)

33 Gutcher, Yell, standing stone 1 HU548985
A modest standing stone of grey gneiss, 1.5m high, overlooks the ferry crossing to Fetlar. The stone shows slight signs of having been worked into shape, rather than just being a natural boulder. (500m S of the ferry terminal, between the road to North Sandwick and the shore. The simplest access route is to drive S 400m on the North Sandwick road, then walk 500m ENE across rough grassland, which can be damp underfoot.)

34 Lumbister, Yell, possible stone rows 1 HU487964 (NOM)
On an area of grass to the east of a ruined sheep pen is a linear setting of small boulders. These are arranged in three parallel lines running from NE to SW; each about 60m long, with the rows spaced about 15m apart. The central line is crossed by a short line of larger boulders, oriented N to S and more closely spaced. This is the only possible example reported in Shetland of a type of monument more common in Caithness. (Park near the Colvister road end, then head W, keeping to higher slopes to the S of Loch of Colvister and Loch of Lumbister. The site lies close to a croft ruin. Rather hard going, for 2.5km.)

35 Windhouse, Yell, chambered cairn 1 HU487917
This heel-shaped cairn has been built on a steep slope, with the façade, built on very large blocks, facing W and downslope. The body of the cairn merges with the slope behind. There is a partly excavated broch by the large ruined house on the hilltop above. (150m N of the bridge on the A968 road at the head of Whale Firth.)

36 Hjaltadans, Stackaberg, Fetlar, circle 1 HU618928
A ring of large boulders surrounds a flat central area, within which is a low circular earthen bank. In the centre are two large upright blocks of stone, standing side by side. The date, period and function of this monument are unknown. (Park at Fetlar airstrip, then walk 750m N.) Important note: site lies in a Special Protection Area that is very important for breeding birds. Between 1 March and 11 August, do not visit before contacting Fetlar-based RSPB Warden on 01957 733 246. Access is usually possible, but Warden has final decision.

37 *Ripple Stone, Fetlar, standing stone 1 HU627905
A 2.3m tall block of schist, this is an unusually slender standing stone for Shetland, being only 1m by 0.4m at the base, and tapering above this. (Between the road and the sea S of Feal.)

38 Skaw Voe, Whalsay, standing stone 2 HU589665 (NOM)
A large boulder, 1.5m high, stands 50m from the SE corner of the bay, and nearby are two fallen or broken stones which once stood taller. (Park before cattle grid, and then walk for 200m downhill towards the sea.)

39 *Pettigarths Field, Yoxie, Whalsay, cairn 2 HU585653
On the rise above the Benie Hoose (2) is a miniature heel-shaped cairn, reduced to its foundation. The cairn has a diameter of only 5m, and the chamber, which is polygonal, is 1m across. It has a narrow passage leading to it from the façade. A cist, possibly a later addition, lies to the N of the chamber, and has at one time been covered by an extension to the cairn. Only a few stones of the covering material remain. (On the rise NW of, and overlooking, the Benie Hoose (2). See that entry for directions.)

40 Brough, Whalsay, cup-marked stone 2 HU555651 (NOM)
Four groups of pecked cup-marks occur on the E side of a rock outcrop. There are at least 30 marks, in four groups. Such cup-marks, believed to be of Bronze Age date, are very rare in Shetland. (On the SE slope of a rock outcrop, directly beyond the end of side road in the township of Houll.)

41 Ward of Symbister, Whalsay, chambered cairn 2 HU533620
A rather ruinous cairn, with traces of a kerb, in a superb location. (Summit of hill, 500m steeply uphill SW of ferry pier – worth the climb for the view as well as the cairn.)

42 Battle Pund, Out Skerries, enclosure 2 HU684713 (NOM)
This irregular setting of large boulders, some 40m across, seems too substantial to be simply the remains an agricultural enclosure. It recalls Hjaltadans (36), and the Doom Rings (56). It may be of Bronze Age date. (From ferry landing point or from airstrip, head W to cross Skerries Bridge onto Housay, take left fork and follow this road S to its end, then walk 200m WSW across open grassland.)

43 *Housetter, North Roe, chambered cairns 3 HU362855
A sadly ruined cairn, with the façade facing E. The overall diameter has

been about 9m, and the inner chamber, of trefoil plan, is 3m by 2 internally. The nearby Giant's Stones are the large upright blocks which are all that survives of the façade of a similar cairn, which has otherwise been completely scattered. High on the rocky hill to the W of the Giant's Stones is a very well preserved, but miniscule, chambered cairn (HU 360855). (Just to the W of the A970 road. The small cairn is only 250m away, but a steep scramble and it requires patience to locate it.)

44 *Ronas Hill, North Roe, chambered cairn 3 HU305835
This, one of the best-preserved chambered tombs in Shetland, stands on the summit of the highest hill in the islands, 450m above sea level. The chamber, which is built of large granite blocks, is still roofed, although much of the cairn material has been scattered over the surrounding slopes. Doubtless the chamber has survived because it provides a shelter in an exposed spot. The interior is rectangular, 1m by 1.25, and 1m high. A remnant of the entrance passage leads into the chamber, and this is the inner end of a formerly longer passage, which led from the outside of a cairn of about 15m in diameter. Its outer end has recently been tampered with and partly "rebuilt". There is little trace of the outer kerb of the cairn, which may have been either round or, more probably, heel-shaped in plan. (Via rapidly deteriorating road to old transmitters on Collafirth Hill, where there is ample parking, or from the head of Ronas Voe. 2.5km by either route, but Collafirth Hill is 200m above sea level, so saves on climb. Not for the unfit or ill-shod, but

excellent for those interested in seeing Shetland's sub-arctic high ground vegetation.)

45 Hamnavoe, Eshaness, standing stones 3 HU243806
"The Giant's Stones" are a pair of upright slabs, one 1.8m tall, the other 2.4m. A third stone, recorded in 1774, has since vanished. The stones lie in an E to W line, but the significance of this is not clear. They may be sailing marks for the bay below. (N of the road, just beside the access to the track leading N to Tingon.)

46 Muckla Water, Eshaness, chambered cairn 3 HU222788
This cairn, also known as the March Cairn, is an almost square example of the heel-shaped type. The remains of a façade can be seen on the N side, framed by uprights, but excavation proved that the small square chamber within was entered not from the façade but from the E side, a most unusual arrangement. (500m N over grass and short heather from the junction of the B9078 and the Priesthoulland road. The March Cairn is the SW of the two shown on the OS 1:50000 map.)

47 *Punds Water, Mangaster, chambered cairn 3 HU325713
This is the best surviving heel-shaped cairn on Mainland and represents an extreme type of plan. The body of the cairn is 15m by 12, and has the outer ends of the façade prolonged into "horns" reminiscent of cairns in Caithness. Within the body of the cairn, and entered from a passage leading from the centre of the concave façade, is a small

rectangular chamber with two alcoves. The main compartment is about 2m square. (750m NW, mainly on steep grass, from the parking place on branch road just E of Mangaster, over a small hill and down to the chambered cairn. The fine house (8) is 500m beyond, around the S shore of Punds Water.)

48 *Islesburgh, chambered cairn
3 HU693685
One of the finest heel-shaped cairns, this was excavated in 1959 and its plan is still very clear. It displays the classic semi-circular form with concave façade. In front of the entrance passage are some stones, which may represent blocking dating from the abandonment of the cairn. The entrance passage leads into a roughly rectangular chamber. All of the slabs which would have roofed the passage and chamber have gone. (Overlooking the shore at Minn, to the W of Mavis Grind. The shortest route, though not easy walking, is to follow the shore 400m NW from Mavis Grind to the head of the bay, then 300m SW to the cairn.)

49 *Busta, Brae, standing stone
3 HU349674
A huge monolith of granite, 3.2m high and about 1.6m wide and broad at the base, stands on the slope of the hill, near to another large block, which may be a fallen companion. The Busta stone is a useful sailing mark, although surely far too large to have been erected solely for that purpose. (E of the road to Busta, just before a cattle grid and opposite some recent houses. The stone is clearly visible from Brae.)

50 Lunning, Lunnasting, standing stone
3 HU506668
A 2m tall stone, of grey conglomerate. (Just beyond the end of the public road.)

51 East Hill of Bellister, chambered cairn
3 HU492592
A probable heel-shaped cairn, with a straight façade on the SE side and a few larger stones, possibly indicating a chamber and passage, within a tumble of smaller stones 10m by 12. (Awkward access, probably the easiest route is to take the track N from Neap to its N end, then strike WNW over the SW shoulder of Northbanks Hill (called Stane Field, not on 1:50000 map), into a valley and on up the opposite slope, maintaining the same direction. Some ruinous but recognisable prehistoric houses are passed just before the top of Stane Field.)

52 *Skellister, South Nesting, standing stone
3 HU463552
A 3m tall standing stone, consisting of an irregular, pointed block of sandstone. Locally called "The Auld Wife", from its resemblance, in silhouette, to a stooped old woman. (Prominent, on a shelf 100m steeply uphill from the junction of the main road and that for Skellister.)

53 *Muckle Ward, Vementry, chambered cairn
3 HU295609
The best preserved of Shetland's heel-shaped cairns, with a diameter of just over 10m, this cairn displays the classic concave façade facing SE and a narrow entrance passage leading to a polygonal chamber. There are traces of two phases of building, with an original round cairn later elaborated to provide a

heel-shaped plan. Interestingly, the entrance passage appears to have been sealed by the façade, suggesting the chamber was already out of use when the heel-shape was introduced. The façade is anchored at each end by rock outcrops. (Summit of hill 1km NW of landing place. This requires private hire or own boat. If visiting Vementry, it is also worth looking at the prehistoric house S of Maa Loch (HU297598) and, much later than our period of interest, the two coastal defence guns and lookout post, still in situ on Swarbacks Head (HU290619) from the last years of World War One.)

54 North Ward of Noonsbrough, chambered cairn   3 HU292579
(NOM – this is not the cairn marked on the OS 1:50000 map, but lies uphill from it, to the E.)
A mound of tumbled rubble marks the site of a heel-shaped cairn, the outer and inner kerbs defined by large blocks of stone and clear traces of a façade to the SE. A more recent watch-tower, now in ruins, lies above the likely location of the chamber of the cairn. (Walk 700m along shore N from road end at Noonsbrough, passing burnt mounds (75) on left and, on the right, the site of a broch, then strike steeply uphill for 200m to reach cairn, on N end of summit ridge.)

55 The Spinner, Sandness, cairn
3 HU215562
This circular cairn, of 8m diameter, seems to have been bounded by a kerb of large blocks. A central cist, 1.4m by 1.1, can be seen, and is built of large slabs. This is probably a Bronze Age cairn, though any finds made when the chamber was dug

out long ago have not survived. (A rough 500m NNE from roadside parking at top of Trona Scord, where road begins to drop steeply towards Sandness.)

56 Doom Rings, Papa Stour
3 HU180603 (NOM)
A setting of close-spaced earth-fast boulders, part buried in sand, lies near the shore at the head of Housa Voe. The horseshoe-shaped setting is open to the E. About 45 boulders are visible, plus a group of 4 set just off-line on the W side. This may be of Bronze Age date, resembling the Battle Pund on Out Skerries (42) – oddly enough, a similar tradition survives here, recalling it as a place where a duel was fought. It may have served as a meeting place during Norse times. On the hill behind is Da Biggings – the site of the principal farm on the island in Norse times. (From ferry landing, walk 600m S along shore and round bay. If arrived by air, walk 500m from airstrip, E then NE along the road toward Da Biggings, take path opposite the house and head downhill for 200m, then leave path and walk N towards shore for 150m. There are several prehistoric house, cairn and burnt mound sites on Papa Stour, and also some fine late mills of Norse type on the W side of the island – if visiting, buy a large-scale map and allow time to explore thoroughly.)

57 Cattapund Knowe, Sandness Road, long cairn   3 HU247516
Under the walls of a group of sheep-pens lie the remains of a long cairn. This has been reduced to a single course of stones, and is somewhat less than impressive, but can be seen

to have measured some 40m by 15. The long cairn may have been made by joining together a pair of round cairns, and traces of a cist can be seen near the southern end. (Close beside the road, immediately W of junction of minor road from Walls and A971 from Bridge of Walls to Sandness.)

58 Gallow Hill, Walls, chambered cairn   3 HU258508
A 10m-diameter cairn, of round plan, with a large cist or ruined chamber in the centre. The central structure, and the edge of the cairn, are built of very large slabs. A second cairn lies to the SW, of similar size but even more badly ruined. (Clearly visible to the N of the A971 road to Walls, 400m beyond the branch to Sandness. Park by roadside and cross 100m of rough grassland.)

59   Ara Clett, Park Hall, Bixter, chambered cairn   3 HU312528
A heel-shaped cairn with a façade on the SSE side, measuring between 15m and 12m across and with the mound of cairn material still about 1m high. Traces of the burial chamber can be made out amongst the rubble. A ruined enclosure nearby is probably recent, though probably built with stones from the cairn. (The cairn is clearly visible from the road. Park beside a track that leaves the N side of the main A971 road 150m W of its junction with the B9071, and walk steeply uphill for 250m.)

60 Wester Skeld, standing stone   4 HU302433
This granite block, 2.8m high and up to 1.9m broad, is of particular interest due to the discovery nearby,

many years ago, of a hoard of six polished stone knives of late Neolithic date. (Park beside the branch road to Scarvister, 500m S of its junction with the road from Easter Skeld to Wester Skeld, and climb steeply up the hill to the W for 400m.)

61   *Murder Stone, Tingwall, standing stone   4 HU412420
A stone 2m high, with a rectangular cross-section, stands immediately beside the road. There is a tale, probably recently invented, which relates a Norse tradition of a pardon for murderers who could run from the Law Ting Holm (128) to the Murder Stone unscathed, against the efforts of the victim's family and friends. (Hard beside the E verge of the road, just N of the Golf Course clubhouse that stands on the opposite side of the road.)

62   Hill of Cruester, Bressay, standing stone   4 HU490428
A 3m high block of sandstone, with a distinct tilt. (From the road between Heogan and Gardie, park near the side road that leads NE uphill, past Keldabister. Just beyond, take the track which heads off NNW for about 600m towards the stone.)

63 Yaa Field, East Burra, standing stone   4 HU378328
A block of gneiss, 2m high and 1m broad, but only 0.15m thick in places, this stone is visible for a considerable distance in most directions. (Park at junction of public road and track to Easter Hogaland, then walk 150m NE up a gentle hill.)

64 Mid Field, West Burra, standing stone 4 HU370326
Of similar height and material to the stone on Yaa Field (63) (which is visible from here), this upright slab is much thicker, being almost square in section. Local legend ascribes to the stone the quality of indestructibility, a power which nature is slowly contradicting. (100m downhill from the road, 500m S of the last house in Bridge-End.)

65 Ward of Scousburgh, chambered cairn 4 HU388188
One of the few surviving prehistoric cairns in the South Mainland, this is a scattered mound of rubble, with clear traces of a kerb defining an original diameter of 9.5m. (On the summit, below the trig point set within the derelict fenced compound of the more SW'ly of the various transmitter stations on the top of the hill. It is possible, at the time of writing, to drive up the access road to the summit of the hill, which offers a superb panoramic view of the whole south end of the Mainland and, on a clear day, as far afield as Noss, Foula and Fair Isle.)

66 *Troswick, standing stone
4 HU408166
A slab of sandstone 2.3m high, this stone stands close beside a field dyke, and may have functioned as a boundary marker, although it is hard to explain why, if this is the case, it is not incorporated in the nearby wall. Its size would suggest that it is of considerable antiquity, and has been used as a landmark, rather than erected to form one. (Park 100m S of the more southerly of two roads leading off the Boddam-Clumlie road down to Troswick, cross the

fence and head ESE for about 400m, keeping an old stone dyke to the left. The stone stands just above the dyke, and appears in view soon after leaving the road.)

Bronze Age – burnt mounds

67 Fairy Knowe, Kettlester, Yell
2 HU511800 (NOM)
One of the few burnt mounds in the North Isles, this example is still quite large, standing almost 2m tall. (Just S of the B9081 road immediately E of Kettlester.)

68 Sweinkatofts, Houbie, Fetlar
2 HU633900 (NOM)
Like Unst and Yell, Fetlar does not appear to have many burnt mounds. Somewhat spread over the centuries by agriculture, this typical example measures about 4m by 6 and less than 1m tall. (Simplest approach is to park by the public road and walk down the access leading towards East House and Aith Ness. This bends sharply left then right. At the right hand bend, head left (E) across field for 100m. The mound lies beside the fence at the N side of the field, near the head of Burn of Ness.)

69 Loch of Sandwick, Whalsay, 2 mounds 2 HU538617
N of the settlement remains described above (4) and prominent by the S shore of the loch is a particularly large burnt mound, standing almost 3m tall. A second, smaller, mound lies 100m to its SE, within the settlement remains. (400m to 600m W from the road, steeply down hill between the Sandwick crofts – numerous fences make this an awkward site to access.)

70 *Burnside, Hillswick
3 HU281784

A large mound of crescentic plan, some 11m across and up to 1m high. At its centre is a well-preserved cooking trough of stone, 1.4m long by 0.6m wide. (50m SW of house: ask for permission and take care when crossing fences.)

71 *Crosskirk, Eshaness
3 HU215780

A large crescentic mound, with the upper edges of two stones of a probable trough visible. (Beside NE shore of Loch of Breakon, 100m S of cattle-grid on road to lighthouse.)

72 Niddister, Hillswick
3 HU278756

A large burnt mound, some 17m by 14 and 1.7m high, with the traces of a ruined cooking trough within the arms of the crescent. (At the W end of a small loch, S of Hillswick, 1km SW of the road end near Findlins in Hillswick village. If visiting this site, it is worth taking in Grevasound prehistoric house (7) and also looking (with care) at the cliffs on the W side of the peninsula, which have steatite outcrops.)

73 Lunna, 3 mounds
3 HU485695, HU484697

A large crescentic burnt mound, over 2m tall, lies close to the shore beside a very small stream course. Further north are two fairly undistinguished but typical small burnt mounds, lying 30m apart in rather damp ground. (The first mound is beside the shore at the N end of the shingle beach. The other pair are reached along the track past Westlea, about 200m NNE from the point where the track ends at the gate into a large field.)

74 *Crawton, Sandness
3 HU214577

A large burnt mound, of kidney-shaped plan, 16m by 12, and 1.5m high, this fine example stands beside a boggy area. There is no sign of a trough. (Park beside the road and walk 50m N along the track which runs on to Ness. The mound is clearly visible to the left (W) of the track.)

75 Noonsbrough, Clousta
3 HU296573 (NOM)

A small example, looking almost like two separate mounds, set in a damp hollow. (To the left (WSW) of the cattle-grid, shortly before the end of the public road at Noonsbrough.)

76 Huxter, Sandness, 2 mounds
3 HU172565, HU173567

Two large burnt mounds are clearly visible from the shore of Loch of Huxter. These burnt mounds are unusual in having acquired names that are not purely locational: respectively the Little and, further S, the Muckle Brownie's Knowes. (Park at public road end at Huxter, and follow farm track SSW for about 400m – the Little Brownie's Knowe lies S of the track, under a modern field wall. A further 400m along the track leads towards the Muckle Brownie's Knowe.)

77 Hockland, Stanydale, 2 mounds
3 HU302513

Two mounds, both over 1.5m high, stand close together S of Hockland. (Park at road junction beside telephone kiosk, then walk 250m along track NE towards Hockland. The mounds lie in the damp area 100m S of the track.)

78 Burn of Setter, Mid Walls, 5 mounds

3 HU210503-HU214508

Five burnt mounds, all in a reasonable state of repair, can be seen scattered up the valley of the burn. (Park where the road crosses the burn, and walk NNE up the burn: the farthest mound is only 300m from the road, the others closer.)

79 Grunivoe, Bridge of Walls, 3 mounds

3 HU250489, HU251486

Typical specimens of burnt mounds, all part way between oval and crescentic in form, and all slightly damaged by grazing animals. (The first mound is 150m NE up the burn that flows from Loch of Grunnavoe into the sea at the Houb. The other two lie close together S of Grunivoe, and can be reached by leaving the public road about 100m S of the cattle-grid and crossing the fenced field in an ENE direction.)

80 *Scord Junction, Scalloway

4 HU408402

This large mound has been rather scattered by agriculture and quarrying, but is still impressive. It can be seen clearly from the main road. (50m W of the B9074 road N to Tingwall, 100m N of its junction with the main A970 Lerwick-Scalloway road.)

81 Cruester, Bressay

4 HU483424

A large oval, 20m by 15, this burnt mound was excavated, many years ago, and has recently been re-examined. It contained a small oval chamber with a corbelled roof. This was possibly part of a domestic building associated with the mound. (On the shore, NW of Gardie House. Approaching downhill from the road, the mound is on the very edge of the shore, to the right of a large ruined building.)

82 Mill Loch, Mousa

4 HU460236

A much-reduced burnt mound stands close beside a stream. It was originally of a horseshoe-shaped plan, but has now degenerated into two curved banks, whose concavities face each other across a central space within which can clearly be seen the edges of the slabs forming the cooking trough. (200m NE of the broch, at the W end of the Mill Loch – see Mousa broch (105) for access details.)

83 *Skelberry, Boddam, 4 mounds

4 HU393163 (NOM)

These mounds lie along a small shallow valley N of the road. The largest, and nearest to the road, stands almost 3m high. (N of the B9122 Boddam to Bigton road, not far from its junction with the main A970 road.)

84 Backasetter, Spiggie

4 HU377156

A large crescentic mound stands in marshy ground at the S end of the Loch of Spiggie, a typical location. (Just N of minor road, immediately to E of Bakkasetter.)

85 Southvoe, Boddam

4 HU398147

A very large burnt mound stands just E of the road. Some large stones protrude slightly from the surface, but these are probably later additions rather than the remains of any Bronze Age structure. (Immediately E of the road a short distance N of the Southvoe Croft Museum. Park at Museum and walk back up road.)

86 Quendale, Sumburgh
4 HU385128

An oval mound some 15m by 8m stands to 2m. It is near to the junction of two very small streams. The rolling grassy basin inland from Quendale Bay was the scene of a several large sand-blows in the mid-late 17th Century, which buried much fertile ground, several farms and a laird's house. (Follow road from Toab NNW to a group of relatively new houses at Hestingsgott. Park here and take track in same direction down towards shore, diverging right onto another track just before the shore is reached. The burnt mound is beyond the end of this track, about 750m in total beyond the road end.)

87 *Houlalie, Pund, Fair Isle, composite mound
4 HZ377156

By far the largest burnt mound in Shetland, this measures 39m by 27m, and stands to 3m in height. It has been dug into in the past, but there is no record of what, if anything, was discovered. The mound seems to be composed of several separate smaller mounds, and probably had several cooking places. (From the road about 300m SW of its junction with the airstrip track, take the track 200m NW to derelict croft buildings at Pund, then 100m NNE to the mound. If starting from the ferry landing, add 1.5km to reach the junction and proceed as above.)

Iron Age – defensive sites

88 Underhoull, Unst, broch & ramparts
1 HP574044

This ruined broch with strong outer defences stands on the edge of a steep slope. The sides not protected by the slope have been enclosed with two ditches, with massive earthen ramparts inside each. The only detail of the broch itself which can be discerned is the outer end of the entrance passage, which is on the north, where a causeway runs through the ramparts, which are faced with stone in this portion of their circuit. A rectangular Norse house, which excavation showed to post-date several Iron Age round houses, lies 200m steeply downslope to the W. (100m W of the public road as it begins to descend into the Westing. Park by roadside and take care with fences.)

89 *Hoga Ness, Belmont, Unst, broch & ramparts
1 HP557006

The broch is completely ruined, but around it are most impressive outer defences. A deep ditch cuts off the angle of coast on which the broch stands. The inner face of this has been edged with a stone wall, which survives best at the western edge of the ditch, beyond the approach causeway on that side. Beyond an outer rampart is a second, shallower, ditch. (Park at ferry terminal at Belmont, walk a short distance N along road then descend W to shore and around beach, climbing onto grassy headland at far side. About 700m from ferry terminal.)

90 *Burgi Geos, Yell, promontory fort
1 HP478034

One of the most spectacular locations of any site in Shetland. An artificial ditch has cut off a promontory formed by two narrow clefts in the cliffs. Beyond the ditch can still be seen the remains of a dry stone structure, including one wall of what may have been a blockhouse similar to that at Scatness North. This wall runs right to the cliff edge on the northern side. On the landward side of the ditch, a pathway runs towards the fort, edged by upright stones set like teeth into a mound of earth. This resembles the device called a *chevaux de frise*, which is usually an extra defence, but here it seems as if intended to prevent those approaching from falling over the cliff. There are traces of fields and clearance cairns on the hill slopes to the E, and these may well be contemporary with the fort. (On the uninhabited W coast of North Yell, and a hard 4km each way. Park at the Gloup Fishermen's Memorial. A path runs from Gloup up the E side of Gloup Voe. From the head of the voe, the route is trackless, SW then W up the valley of Rule's Gill, over Hill of Vigon and down to the coast.)

91 *Burra Ness, Yell, broch
1 HU557957
Only the seaward portion of this broch has survived, but this still reaches 3m above ground level. At the S end of the visible remains is the wreck of a wall-base cell, perhaps once a guard cell. The broch has been protected on the landward side by a pair of earthen ramparts, and there are many small foundations within these. Behind the broch, the flat, rather boggy land is dotted with many clearance cairns. (Road to North Sandwick, then track S, then E, out to headland. 2km from North Sandwick.)

92 Stoal, Aywick, Yell, promontory fort
1 HU546873
This is a miniature bivallate (double-ditched) fort, with three ramparts and two ditches. The ramparts stand up to 1.8m in height. The enclosed area has been somewhat eroded, but can never have been very large. So far as can be seen, the ramparts are made solely of earth and small stones. (Park at Aywick, then follow path ENE for 1km past ruined croft of Stoal. Take care to keep back from edge of cliffed inlet just before fort.)

93 Snabrough, Fetlar, fort
1 HU577933
This badly eroded fort has been claimed as a former broch site, on no good evidence. A last fragment of masonry, probably part of a blockhouse, is flanked on the shoreward side by two substantial banks and broad ditches. Pottery has been found in the shoreline section. (Drive S for 1km from ferry terminal, park by roadside and head W for 500m, to reach the coast just S of headland.)

94 Houbie, Fetlar, broch
1 HU620903
The foundations of a broch, 18m in outer diameter, stand on a low platform flanked by a broad ditch and outer bank. A second bank is apparent on the NW side, where the approach is easiest. Medieval steatite workings lie on the edge of low cliffs 150m WSW of the broch. (The best approach is to park by road and cross roadside fence by bend in road a short distance E of where it crosses West Burn of Houbie, then head 200m S, keeping close to fence on W side of field.)

Gazetteer

95 Aithbank, Fetlar, promontory fort 1 HU642897
The promontory called Winna Tanga is crossed by three much-reduced rubble banks, and is almost certainly a promontory fort. (Park near cattle-grid just E of Aithbank, then head 250m SSW keeping beside old dyke. This brings you to the shore E of the fort, with a good view of it. Take care if venturing onto the promontory itself.)

96 Loch of Huxter, Whalsay, fort 2 HU558620
An islet has been connected to the S shore by a rubble causeway. Where the causeway reaches the islet, a small blockhouse, now ruined, once stood. This is recorded, last century, as standing over 2m tall, with an upper gallery in the wall. The rest of the islet is edged by a stone wall some 1.5m thick, and the join between it and the blockhouse suggests the wall was built after the blockhouse, although not necessarily long after. (Park on public road to W of Loch of Huxter, at point where access track to water pumping station leaves the road. Skirt around the W and SW shore for about 600m to reach the point where the causeway heads into the loch. Causeway is very insecure – be prepared for wet feet or worse.)

97 *Loch of Houlland, Eshaness, broch 3 HU213793
This rubble-filled broch stands above encircling debris, probably to about 3.5m above its original ground level. The entrance is in the SW side, and has had a guard cell on the right. Two ruined cells can be seen in the wall foundations. A stone-faced bank has cut off the promontory on which the broch stands. Within this enclosed area there are, as well as the broch, a number of oval and sub-rectangular foundations, some of which are later than the broch. A nearby island is joined to the shore and to the broch by causeways, and may have served as a place of safety for livestock. (Park 500m before Esha Ness lighthouse, level with the head of a long cliff-edged inlet, then walk 500m NE across short grass to reach the W end of Loch of Houlland, from which the broch is a further 250m around the loch's NW shore.)

98 Burga Water, Lunnasting, dun 3 HU481641
A small dun occupies an islet. Drystone walling can be seen on the S and E sides. (The islet is towards the S end of the loch, and is best viewed from the minor road that passes above the E shore of the loch.)

99 Hog Island, North Nesting, promontory fort 3 HU508581
This promontory fort has been cut off by the sea. Three slight ramparts are preserved on the landward side of a narrow channel, which has been eroded by the sea but was probably originally a natural dip. There is a central entrance gap in the ramparts. (Park at Neap, walk downhill 250m E to bay and follow the shore E for a further 500m.)

100 *Ness of Garth, Sandness, promontory fort 3 HU216583
A promontory fort (now made into a tidal island by rising sea level) is protected by two stone-faced ramparts on the landward side. A less stoutly built wall runs along the W side. There are small oval house

foundations inside the fort, and these appear to be of later date, perhaps representing a monastic establishment. (Park near gate to track which leaves the public road just E of a public telephone kiosk and follow track NNE, swinging briefly E as it crosses a small burn at the N end of the loch, towards the old croft of Ness, beyond which the fort lies on the headland to the N.)

101   *Burga Water, Sandness Road, dun   3 HU234539
A fine example of an island dun, preserved due to its inaccessibility. Partly tumbled stonework rings a small island, and survives well enough to suggest a circular plan and a wall 2m thick surrounding a 10m-diameter interior. In places the wall stands 2m high. There is no trace of a former causeway. (Clearly visible in loch about 600m to NE of the A971 Sandness road as it crosses the E shoulder of Stourbrough Hill at HU228536 – park here and view from roadside.)

102 *Culswick, broch
                    4 HU253448
Two centuries ago this was the second highest surviving broch in Shetland, but has since been reduced to about 4m in height. There is a small chamber above the entrance passage, which is on the SE, entered from within the broch, and a gallery has run within the wall at the same height as this chamber. A guard cell opens off the right hand side of the entrance passage. The blocky red granite of which the broch is constructed seems to have required unusual building techniques. A large triangular lintel over the outer end of the entrance

passage seems designed to spread the load away from the rather poorly built passage roof, and instead of the more normal internal ledge or scarcement to support internal wooden structures and the roof, there are several projecting blocks spaced around the inside wall face about 3m above the original floor level. (Park beside telephone kiosk at Culswick. Take track WNW towards chapel, then W past N end of Sand Water and WSW to the ruined croft of Sotersta. From Sotersta, head W to reach the S end of Loch of Culswick, and then NNW up the far side to the broch, which stands at the N end of rising ground. 1.7km from the roadside to the broch. In passing, note the small standing stone at Sotersta, embedded in a ruined outbuilding.)

103 Noss Sound, Bressay, broch & ramparts   4 HU528410
A large mound partly conceals the ruined broch. Traces of cells are visible within the walls. Two substantial ramparts flank the mound. These appear to be earthen, but recent marine erosion has shown that one, at least, conceals a stone-faced wall. The location is unusual for a broch, being overlooked by nearby high ground. (Park at the road end, and walk downslope to the Noss ferry point.)

21a   *Clickimin, Lerwick, fort, broch & houses   4 HU464408
The Bronze Age unenclosed settlement consisting of a small oval house and outbuildings was replaced by a series of Iron Age defensive constructions before the site ended its use as a late Iron Age /

Pictish period settlement. The complex sequence of two or three partial re-buildings of a simple fort, with wooden lean-to buildings around its inner wallface, followed by the addition of a freestanding blockhouse, perhaps part of an uncompleted rebuilding of the defences, and finally a broch, is unique. The site was excavated, badly, in the 1850s and again, to a higher standard, in the late 1950s and early 1960s. Guardianship monument, no charge. See also Historic Scotland guidebook. (Signposted, to right of A970 road leaving Lerwick for the S.)

104 *Burland, Quarff, broch & ramparts   4 HU445360
A broch with later internal structures stands on a promontory. To the landward side are three earthen ramparts, which were probably faced in stone. These are substantial enough to have constituted a defence on their own, and but for the broch this site would be classed as a promontory fort. The broch entrance is less than 1m from the cliff edge. Within the broch are traces of later structures, similar to the arrangement at Clickimin (21a) whereby the interior was narrowed to take a single house at ground level. (The easiest route, avoiding the worst of the boggy ground and fences, is from the A970 about 500m S of the access to Brindister Quarry. Head E for about 800m to the head of the inlet just W of the broch, round the N end of this and climb the steep grassy slope past a ruined croft to the broch. Take care at the unfenced cliff edge. It is possible to park at Loch of Brindister and follow the stream valley towards

the coast, climbing a little on the N side of the valley to head direct for the broch, but this route is boggy, is little shorter and has more fences to cross.)

105 *Mousa, broch   4 HU456237
This is the best-preserved broch of all, and stands over 13m tall, little short of its original height. (Although it was repaired in the mid 19th century, it was not heightened at this time.) The base of the tower is unusually narrow, being just over 15m wide externally with walls 4.5m thick, making Mousa the most massively-built of any broch so far measured. The basal level is pierced by a narrow entrance, with no guard cells. In the wallbase are three oval cells, entered by narrow doorways from the central area. These have beehive-corbelled roofs. The stairway starts at a raised aperture 2m above the broch floor and rises spirally through the hollow wall to the wallhead, where it opens onto a partially roofed upper gallery. Within the double-skinned wall are six galleries, floored and roofed by lintels, which also serve to tie the inner and outer walls together. These are difficult to reach from the stairway, as this cuts through them, necessitating a gap in each gallery floor. The inner face of the broch has long, vertical, gaps in the masonry, broken by spaced tie-stones. These "voids" allow light into the galleries, lighten the structure and may also have served, in conjunction with the two ledges, which protrude from the inner face, to support a wooden structure of galleried form and a roof. On the floor of the broch is a rock-cut tank for water and a hearth, over which project the remains of a

wheelhouse-like building that was inserted at a later date. Outside the broch are slight traces of outbuildings, contained within a stone wall, which runs across the neck of the promontory on which the broch stands. Note also the burnt mound (82) and a fine ruined Norse-type mill between the broch and Mill Loch. Guardianship monument. See also Historic Scotland guidebook. (By boat – charge – from Sand Lodge pier, landing on flat rocks at Mousa, then a 700m walk over grass to the broch. Contact Tourist Office or telephone 01950 431364 for details and to book – the boat normally operates to a pre-published schedule from late May to early September, is weather-dependent and can be busy in fine weather during July and early August.)

106 Clumlie, broch   4 HU404181
This broch, revealed by excavation in the late 19th century, stands in the centre of a group of croft buildings which are themselves of interest and illustrates how even so large a structure as a broch can be subsumed in later remains and concealed. The broch at Clumlie stands to just over 2m in height, and is of similar proportions to that at Jarlshof (25). Part of the outer wall has been removed. There is a guard cell to the right of the narrow entrance, while a cell on the left may have led to a stair. On the floor of the broch can be seen the outline of a hearth and stone subdivisions which may be original fittings of the broch or later modifications. A later wall has been inserted, around the inner face of the broch wall, narrowing the interior diameter.

(Park beside road S of access to Braefield, by gate leading to a track on W side of road and follow this track 200m W to a cluster of ruined croft buildings.)

107 Dalsetter, Boddam, broch & ramparts   4 HU408157
Only a mound of rubble remains of the broch, but its surrounding ramparts are still impressive. Two earthen banks stand up to 3m tall, and between them is a broad flat-bottomed ditch. A gap in these defences, on the SE, probably marks the original approach. The remains form a prominent landmark for many miles, and the site is known as "da Brough", in preference to all the other local brochs, which are simply named after their locality. Whether this indicates an Iron Age importance, or simply the prominence of the site, is not known. (Park near Dalsetter farm and head 500m SE along a rough track towards the prominent mound on the skyline.)

108   *Old Scatness, Sumburgh, broch and houses   4 HU390106
This complex comprises a broch surrounded by the most extensive assemblage of late Iron Age / Pictish period buildings so far excavated in Shetland (see below). The broch was discovered during airport improvements in 1974, and although it now lies on the edge of the site, it is possible that it was once central to a larger array of buildings, which were reduced unrecorded in earlier airport works. Excavation of the broch produced early dates (around 300 BC) for its construction, and the site as a whole has required changes to many ideas about the middle and late Iron Age / Pictish period. At

present the site is being consolidated for visitors, following major excavations from 1995 to 2004. Site with small visitor centre open (charge) during summer months. Contact Tourist Office or Shetland Amenity Trust 01595 694688 for details. (Park by seaward side of main road just S of airport runway and emergency access road and take great care crossing the road. Access arrangements are likely to change as the site is developed over the next few years.)

25a *Jarlshof, Sumburgh, broch & houses   4 HU399096

The broch lies at the centre of the coastal side of this complex site. It has been neatly halved by marine erosion, and affords an unusual opportunity to see a broch in section. The remaining half of the broch stands well over 2m high. The outer diameter was 19m, with walls 5m thick at the base. The broch entrance passage has a guard cell, but any stair has gone with the vanished half of the structure. An outer wall, enclosing a courtyard around the broch entrance, was found to be contemporary with the broch, and was provided with an entrance containing a guard cell. This outer wall probably marks a stage of development beyond the ring-wall at Clickimin (21a), and its occurrence at the same date as a fully-developed broch may call into doubt the sequence at Clickimin. Guardianship monument, visitor centre open during summer only, admission charge. Contact 01950 460112 (out-of-season, 01856 841815). See also Historic Scotland guidebook. (Signposted, parking at Sumburgh Hotel.)

109 Scatness North, Sumburgh, promontory fort   4 HU388087

On the headland NNE of Ness of Burgi (110) is a fort, which was excavated in 1983. It proved to have a rectangular masonry blockhouse with a single oval cell in the surviving half, and an entrance passage with a door-check and a bar-hole halfway down. At the back of the blockhouse, protruding stones formed a stair, which was incorporated in a later modification that thickened the structure, perhaps to allow it to stand higher. On the landward side of the promontory is a rampart with a broad, irregular, ditch, the latter more like a quarry scoop than a defensive feature. (Park at end of public road, taking care not to block the bus turning space. Then walk 700m S over open grassland. The fort lies on the left (E), before the dip down to the beach preceding Ness of Burgi.)

110 *Ness of Burgi, Sumburgh, promontory fort   4 HU388085

This is the classic example of a Shetland blockhouse fort. It was excavated in the 1930s and has been laid out for visitors. A double ditch with intervening rampart cuts off a promontory. A paved and stone-faced passage, possibly originally roofed, leads through this outer defence towards a rectangular block of masonry, pierced by a narrow entrance passage. A guard cell lies to the left of the passage, and two further cells lie to the right, entered from the rear of the blockhouse. The plan is interesting, for the blockhouse does not reach to the cliff edge on the N side, and there is no trace of a wall there. Also, no trace of any other buildings was found within the enclosed area, not even against the rear face of the blockhouse. It is thought that the blockhouse, which now stands about 2m high, was originally at least twice that height, with a wallhead walkway fronted by a parapet, but this is pure conjecture, based on the volume of tumbled stone removed by the excavators, and stacked neatly nearby. Guardianship monument, un-restricted access. See also Historic Scotland guidebook. (Park at end of public road, taking care not to block the bus turning space. Then walk 800m S over open grassland, passing the fort at Scatness North (109) on the left before a short descent to a small shingle beach and a final short easy scramble over sloping rocks and a further 200m on grass to the fort.)

111 *Landberg, Fair Isle, promontory fort 4 HZ223722
A cliffed promontory is protected on the landward side by steep ramparts with intervening ditches, enclosing a small flat area. Recent excavation revealed the foundations of a small forgotten Medieval chapel just within the inner rampart, overlying remains of a possible Iron Age gatehouse to the fort. The ditches were sectioned, and proved to be considerably deeper than they now appear. Iron Age and later finds were recovered, but the interior had suffered badly from burrowing rabbits and puffins. (Directly in front of the Fair Isle Bird Observatory building at North Haven. 200m SW along road from ferry landing. From the airstrip, S to the road then NE along this to the Observatory: just under 1km in total.)

Later Iron Age / Pictish domestic sites

112 Wadbister, Bressay, souterrain 4 HU516395
This souterrain, or earth-house, is a typical Shetland example, being well-built but small, cramped and rather hard to locate. It is frequently damp, making the crawl down the surviving 1.5m of roofed entrance passage awkward. The oval inner chamber is about 2m long, 1.5m wide and 1m high – not for the claustrophobic. There is a burnt mound 100m to the SW. (Park at the N end of Loch of Brough, then take the track on the W side of the loch 1.2km SSE, past the W end of Loch of Grimsetter, then head 250m SE to the ruined croft on the saddle S of the loch. The souterrain is beside the croft ruins.)

21b *Clickimin, Lerwick, fort, broch & houses 4 HU464408
Following Bronze Age domestic and Iron Age defensive phases, the subsequent disuse of the defensive elements was marked by a reduction of the diameter of the interior to form a single house, and the erection of a number of small sub-circular buildings within the fort wall but outside the broch. A possibly late, and potentially very important, feature is a stone slab set on the approach causeway across the marshy land outside the broch and marked with the carved shape of two footprints. Elsewhere in northern and western Britain such stones are often associated with kingship rituals. The site was excavated, badly, in the 1850s and to a higher standard in the late 1950s and early 1960s.

Guardianship monument, no charge. See also Historic Scotland Guidebook. (Signposted, to right of A970 road leaving Lerwick for the S.)

108a *Old Scatness, Sumburgh, broch and houses   4 HU390106
This complex comprises a broch (see above) surrounded by the most extensive assemblage of late Iron Age / Pictish period buildings so far excavated in Shetland. This is made more remarkable still by the existence less than 1km away of a second, almost equally complex, site at Jarlshof (25b, below). Old Scatness' post-broch buildings include a wheelhouse, and several roundhouses of varied design, the whole spanning the period from the broch to the Norse settlement. Fragments of Pictish-style carving have come from the site (in the Shetland Museum, Lerwick). Replicas of a Pictish smith's house and a wheelhouse have been constructed alongside the excavated area. At present the site is being consolidated for visitors, following major excavations from 1995 to 2004. Site with small visitor centre open (charge) during summer months. Contact Tourist Office or Shetland Amenity Trust 01595 694688 for details. (Park by seaward side of main road just S of airport runway and emergency access road and take great care crossing the road. Access arrangements are likely to change as the site is developed over the next few years.)

25b. *Jarlshof, Sumburgh, broch & houses   4 HU399096
The post-broch phase at Jarlshof was marked by rapid accumulation of wind-blown sand, in a series of layers, with over 2m of accumulation and midden deposits of similar depths around the remains of the broch. The result is a very deep stratigraphy, and there are doubtless remains of many periods on this site, both in unexcavated parts and where the earlier excavators stopped at relatively late, high, levels. Even so, the complex of post-broch structures at Jarlshof is one of the most remarkable in Scotland. The broch was closely followed by a stone roundhouse, built within the outer enclosure of the broch. This was followed by three wheelhouses, one of which was built within the broch itself. Two of the wheelhouses survive almost intact, with roofs corbelled inwards to leave a small central hole, which would have been easy to roof with thatch. These structures, so far as they can be dated by their form and finds, seem to have evolved on site, but the claim of the excavator that Jarlshof marked the point of birth of the wheelhouse architectural style seems hard to reconcile with the predominantly Hebridean distribution of this building form. After the wheelhouses, a series of sunken-floored, sub-circular houses was built, associated with two small souterrains, or earth-houses, which were probably underground stores. These houses may have been built of turf, with only stone foundations. Even later is a small house with a kiln-barn, which stands to the W of the main complex. A group of poorly-preserved circular houses of this period lay directly under the Norse settlement (see below) but these are not visible on the site as laid out. These last houses may have been inhabited at the date of the

first Norse settlement. Guardianship monument, visitor centre open during summer only, admission charge. Contact 01950 460112 (out-of-season, 01856 841815). See also Historic Scotland guidebook. (Signposted, parking at Sumburgh Hotel, then 200m surfaced path to site.)

Early Christian sites

113 Burgar Stack, Unst, eremitic site 1 HU661140 (NOM)
Slight traces of small house foundations are located on this exposed stack, which is linked to the shore by a dangerous rock ridge. (Do not attempt access, but view from the safety of the hill above. Park at Norwick cemetery and walk E to end of road, then continue in the same direction to reach the coast about one-third of the way up its rise to the Horns of Hagmark. About 1km from cemetery.)

114 Blue Mull, Unst, eremitic site 1 HP557045 (NOM)
On a headland above steep cliffs may be seen seven oblong building foundations, arranged in a straight line. The headland has been delimited by a low bank, which seems unlikely ever to have been high enough to act as a defence. (Park at Old Kirk of Lund and walk directly WNW for 1km, or take the slightly longer but more scenic route skirting the coast, first N then W.)

115 Birrier of West Sandwick, Yell, eremitic site 1 HU438913
Facing Kame of Isbister (116) across Yell Sound, this almost inaccessible sloping promontory, linked to Yell by a rock ridge, has two rows of small dwelling foundations, and seems more likely to be an eremitic settlement than anything else, given its location. (Another site with dangerous access. It can be viewed from the nearby cliff edge. Take N access road to West Sandwick, then the right fork to Harkland. Park beside (not blocking) entrance to track on right, which leads first W then NNW for 1.5km past Mill Loch. Beyond this a path continues in the same direction for a further 500m to Loch of Birriesgirt. A short steep climb NW beyond the N end of the loch brings one to the cliff edge at a point overlooking the site.)

116 *Kame of Isbister, North Roe, eremitic site 1 HU382915
On a steeply sloping promontory above Yell Sound, facing Birrier of West Sandwick (115) are the remains of 23 small sub-rectangular foundations, each one about 3m by 6. They are arranged in two rows. The area with the buildings faces E, and the buildings cannot be seen from the adjacent shore. (The only approach is by a crumbling rock ridge, and is not safe. To view the spectacular site from the shore nearby, walk 1km E from Isbister past a small loch, skirting this on the N side, to the cliff edge, from where there is a good view NNE to the site.)

117 The Clett, Fetlar, eremitic site 1 HU642945 (NOM)
Extreme even by Shetland stack-site standards, a cluster of tiny building ruins perches on this sheer-side, sloping-topped rock off the N cliffs of Fetlar. (Inaccessible, unless one has a helicopter, but there is a good distant view from the Yell-Unst ferry

crossing. The nearest point on the shore of Fetlar is a long 4km from the road, from the airstrip N to the summit of Vord Hill (chambered cairns) and then ENE to Busta Hill. (See important note about access at Gazetteer entry 1.) Alternatively, from the public road 500m E of Aith, head N up track to deserted croft of Still, then up the Burn of Aith, on past the ruined croft of Mongirsdale to Loch of Winyadepla and up Busta Hill from its S side. Both routes are fascinating walks through unfrequented moorland.)

118   Kebister, Dales Voe, early church site and other remains
4 HU457455 (NOM)
Excavated between 1985 and 1987, this site produced evidence of occupation from prehistoric times up to the Iron Age. After a hiatus in the record, evidence was found, in the form of foundation trenches, for what was almost certainly a small chapel, along with two 10th century graves. Finds (in Shetland Museum, Lerwick) included a small stone with a simple cross incised on it, and a fragment of exotic porphyry with early Christian associations. The large rectangular building which is the main feature visible on site is an early 16th century teind (tithe) barn, erected for the Archdeacon of Shetland, suggesting that this site may have retained its ecclesiastical association over the intervening centuries. (From main road N out of Lerwick, take the side road on the right (soon to be access for Bressay Bridge) past Green Head industrial site and incinerator, swinging N then NW before dropping down to industrial site at road end. Park before the gates of the compound and cross field fence on right, passing some small burnt mounds to skirt around outside the compound on its SE side. The site lies at the W end of the industrial site, just outside its boundary fence. 200m from the road end to the site.)

119   Cullingsburgh, Bressay, church site   4 HU522423
The remains of a cruciform Medieval church, dedicated to St Mary, lie within an old graveyard, under the NW corner of which lie the much reduced foundations of a broch. A very fine Pictish cross-slab found near the church has one of the few ogham inscriptions so far found in Shetland. The stone is now in the National Museum in Edinburgh. (Road to Setter, park near junction with a track on the right and follow this track to the NE, then for 800m along the shore to the E, passing a burnt mound near the end of the track and then the ruins of Cullingsburgh croft before the graveyard is reached.)

120 Papil, West Burra, church site
4 HU368315
The large post-Reformation church at Papil, itself disused, stands on a low mound which represents the site of at least one earlier church, dedicated to St Laurence. This, together with the church on St Ninian's Isle (121), may have been one of the principal churches of southern Shetland in pre-Norse times and possibly later. Nothing can be seen on site from this period apart from a curved bank, which may be part of an enclosure associated with the early church. The churchyard has produced a remarkable group of Pictish

sculptured stones that seem to span a long period of time. Among the earlier pieces is the "Papil Stone", a cross slab bearing an incised pattern including a lion and two bird-headed men, and equally impressive is the "Monks' Stone", the side slab of an altar or shrine which depicts a procession of four clerics, one mounted on a small horse. This has what may be the earliest known depiction of a Shetland pony. A number of other fragments suggest that, in its original form, this site was a circular enclosure with a small chapel towards the centre, SE of the present church, and several open-air shrines dotted about the enclosed area. There must be much more remaining on this site than is apparent, for the level of the ground has built up since the period in which the first church was built, perhaps as early as the 8th century. The major stones are in the Museum of Scotland, Edinburgh, with good replicas in the Shetland Museum, Lerwick. (Immediately beside the road, park as for cemetery.)

121 *St Ninian's Isle, Bigton, church site   4 HU368208
Excavations in the late 1950s showed that the ruins of the church overlie an earlier one, within the floor of which was found the famous St Ninian's treasure, a collection of many items of Pictish silverware: bowls, brooches and other ornaments. (It is worth noting that the stone-lined pit within the ruins is not the site of the treasure discovery, but merely shows the depth of the floor of the primary chapel below the later one.) The earliest use of all appears to have been as an Iron Age farmstead, although almost all traces

of this period were destroyed by subsequent ecclesiastical building. The first church was a simple rectangular chapel set within a circular enclosure. Associated with it were some fine carved stones in the Pictish style, including a post-and-slab shrine lying S of the chancel. The later church, the ruins of which can be seen, is probably 12th or 13th century in date. Although there is little documented history for this site it must have been one of the principal churches in pre-Norse Shetland. Recently there has been some reconsideration of the Ninianic dedication, formerly believed to be a late one. The church was recognised as a holy place long after its disuse, and in the late 1700s disapproving ministers of the reformed church wrote of candles being lit at the ruined altar. (Signposted track from near Bigton shop down to the shore. Park here and walk for 700m across the remarkable beach. The chapel is a stiff climb NW up the sandy slope at the far end of the beach, and sits within a fenced and gated enclosure. If the track is closed to vehicles, as sometimes happens, park at the shop and walk along the track instead – this adds about 500m each way.)

Viking/Norse

122 Hamar, Baltasound, Unst, house   1 HP646093 (NOM)
One of a number of Norse period houses recently recorded in Unst, this fine example displays the characteristics well – elongated rectangular plan, aligned up- and down-slope, with side walls bowed outwards. The house stands within an enclosure which may represent

the "homefield" of the farm, and unusually seems to have been abandoned in medieval times, rather than continuing on as a croft until more recently. (The easiest access is probably to take the branch road to the parking area for Keen of Hamar Nature Reserve, then strike directly ESE over the S shoulder of the hill (projecting the line of the access road gives the correct direction), to drop down the far slope above this site, which stands overlooking an extensive flat, boggy area.)

123 Sandwick, Unst, house
1 HP618023 (NOM)
A late Norse house, proven by excavation, this ruined rectangular farmstead dates to around 1300 AD, but in its location at the back of the beach and its layout, with a main building and nearby byre, all within an enclosed yard, it reflects the Norse influence on later Shetland farm arrangements which began with the Viking settlement. The site was excavated in the late 1970s. One of the most interesting features was a "cow-shaped" doorway aperture, narrow at the bottom and widening upwards. This finally explained the problem that the foundation dimensions of the doorways of excavated Norse byres always seemed too narrow for cattle to pass through. A Pictish period burial, dated to about 400 AD, was excavated nearby. It lay below a rectangular cairn of quartz pebbles, which has been replaced and can still be seen. (Park beside the road at the track leading to Hannigarth then walk 500m N, past the croft, to descend to the S end of the sandy bay, where the remains of this site are obvious.)

32a Breakon, Yell, burial
1 HP528053 (NOM)
Near to a rather ruinous oval house, probably prehistoric, is a pointed-oval, or boat-shaped, setting of flat slabs protruding from the sandy soil. This may be the remains of a Viking-period burial. Local traditions of burial nearby, including tales of a "horned man" appear to be associated with the rather larger mounds nearer the shore, which are probably prehistoric. (Follow track from Breakon Farm 350m down to shore, heading for sandy bay.)

124 Gossabrough, Yell, houses
1 HU534833
(OS map marks "broch")
To the N and E of the mound formed by a ruined broch are the remains of several rectangular structures that may represent Norse dwellings. If this is the case, the settlement could be almost as extensive as that of Jarlshof. (Parking is tight at the end of the side road which leads to the delightfully named Bottom, at the east side of the bay, and it is better to park at the beach then follow track E above the bay and up just to the N of Bottom. The broch is the prominent mound about 100m beyond.)

125 Strandburgh, Fetlar, possible monastic site
1 HU670930
(On map as *settlement*)
This seems to be a monastic site. The remains look Norse rather than pre-Norse in date, although there may be a hidden earlier phase. It has two elements, which were possibly once linked by a bridge or natural causeway. On the Outer Brough, a detached stack, are the remains of long houses with slightly bowed

walls. The buildings on the stack may represent the monastic centre, while similar ones on the main island may represent a farm that helped support the community. From here there is a good view of the Clett (117) an almost inaccessible stack 3km to the W, which has small ruins which may be earlier in date or else a hermitage founded from the main centre. (Park at road end at Everland, then 2km NNE over fairly open ground to the very end of the island. It is best to keep to the higher ground.

126 Giants Grave, Aith, Fetlar, burial 1 HU638899 (NOM)
A grass-grown oval mound of stones, about 10m by 5, lies on the edge of the low cliff above the shore. One local tradition, recorded in 1900, tells of a giant, buried with his money below his head and his boat turned upside-down over him. Another tells simply of a dying man who was washed ashore in his boat, and asked to be buried in proper Viking style. Fragments of iron recovered in the 1930s proved to be rivets typical of those used on Viking boats. This appeared to be the only firm contender for a Viking boat-burial so far identified in Shetland. This identification was confirmed in 2002 when the Channel 4's "Time Team" archaeologists excavated the site, finding more boat rivets and a fine tortoise brooch. The brooch suggests that the burial was female, rather than male – although it is not unknown for small family groups to be placed together in boat burials. It appeared that the boat may have been buried beneath a mound of stones because the topsoil was too thin to dig a hole and place it below

ground level, as was more normal. The site has been restored to its previous appearance. (Overlooking Wick of Aith, on the W side of the bay. Most easily reached from the road at the head of Wick of Aith, parking there and walking SW along the top of the steep coastal slope for about 250m.)

127 Kirk Holm, Sand, monastic site 4 HU337460
(On map as *settlement*)
Another site, like Birrier of West Sandwick (115) and Kame of Isbister (116), with a row of several buildings, but here the structures are much larger, being up to 11m in length. They stand parallel, end-on to the shore, towards the E side of the island. This seems most likely to be a Norse period site, similar to Strandburgh (125) or the Peerie Brough at Birsay in Orkney, rather than an ecclesiastical site of Pictish date. The name of the island seems to confirm the church link, although local tradition attributes the foundations to houses built by shipwrecked sailors of the Spanish Armada in 1588. (At the N end of this elongated island, most easily seen from the Reawick road, to the W. For the real enthusiast, a better vantage point is Kirka Ness, reached by parking on the hill above Sand and walking S for 1km.)

128 *Law Ting Holm, Tingwall, thingstead 4 HU417435
The mound at the N end of the loch is traditionally pointed out as the meeting place of the senior legislative assembly for all of Shetland, the *Ting* or *Thing*, in the years preceding the Scottish takeover of the islands. An old path

seems to have led straight downhill from the site where Tingwall church stands and across a causeway through marshy ground to a natural knoll, which is almost surrounded by water. It is reported that until the 18th century large stones formed seats for the participants. Such a location, where the deliberations of the assembly could be seen by onlookers, but not necessarily overheard, is typical of thingstead sites throughout the area settled by the Vikings – the two most famous – and still in ceremonial use – being Thingvellir in Iceland and Tynwald in the Isle of Man. (Probably best viewed from the roadside to the W of the head of the loch, where there is parking. The 150m walk around the head of the loch to the Holm invariably involves wet feet, and there is little to see on site.)

129 *Burn of Catpund, Cunningsburgh, steatite quarries
4 HU426272 (NOM)

The largest outcrop of steatite in the British Isles occupies an E-facing bowl on the hillside. Some fine examples of soapstone working survive, with chisel-marks preserved on many faces and the impressions where bowls and troughs have been prised free. Most, if not all, of the visible workings are medieval rather than Viking in date. A small area of carved rock has recently been exposed, and shows to good advantage the intensive nature of the working of the rock face. Heavy autumn rain a few years ago caused large mud flows from the slopes above, which have scarred the upper hillslopes, exposing fresh outcrops and concealing others. (About 1km S of South Brig of Cunningsburgh, a

cut-off section of old road to the W of the main A971 allows parking. Access is across a simple stile. An unsurfaced informal path winds uphill alongside or above the N bank of the Burn of Catpund for about 300m past several worked outcrops. The area recently excavated is fenced and provided with an information board, which can be seen from downhill. To reach it involves crossing the burn. Do so as far upstream as possible, and take care generally – the grass is often very slippery.)

25c *Jarlshof, Sumburgh, houses
4 HU399096

The extensive Viking period and later remains at Jarlshof represent a long sequence of habitation, from the first Norse settlement perhaps in the early 800s AD through a later village and medieval farm, and ending with a substantial dwelling of late 16th century date. The original settlement seems to have been of one or more very large long halls, which were subsequently modified, sub-divided and added to, resulting in a warren of buildings. While this site has huge archaeological importance, it must be admitted that it is not easy to understand the Viking-Norse sequence from the remains as laid out on the ground, although some recurrent features are clear, such as the central hearths and side-benches of the earlier houses. What the site does convey well is the slow transformation from Viking hall through to Medieval farmhouse, a development which charts the origins of the long crofthouses which until recently were the standard rural dwelling in Shetland. Guardianship monument, visitor centre open during summer only, admission charge. Contact 01950 460112 (out-of-season, 01856 841815). See also Historic Scotland guidebook. (Signposted, parking at Sumburgh Hotel, then 200m surfaced path to site.)

Tours

LERWICK and SCALLOWAY

Starting point: in the centre of Lerwick. Take the main A970 road S (signposted for Sumburgh). Clickimin (21), a complex site with a broch, fort and prehistoric house, is on the right near the large modern leisure centre. Continue on the main road to the public hall at Sound on the left of the road. From here it is a 1km walk S along the slope above the shoreline to the prehistoric house at Punds Geo (22). Back on the road, a further 4km S is a parking area on the right, beside loch of Brindister, with a small circular fortification – in archaeological terms a "dun" – on an islet (HU433370). To the E, silhouetted against the sea, is the broch of Burland (104). It is possible to reach the broch from here down the Brindister Burn, which has some fine ruined mills, but the route can be very damp, with many fences to cross. A more comfortable route to the broch starts a short distance S, parking beside the small loch on the right of the road (Harry's Loch) and then crossing the road to head NE along the heathery ridge and then N up the coast – a distance of about 1km.

Back at the car, turn round and head N again, taking the recently improved road which branches left and follow it toward Scalloway. There is parking with a splendid view over the small town, Shetland's medieval "capital". The well-preserved shell of the late 16th century

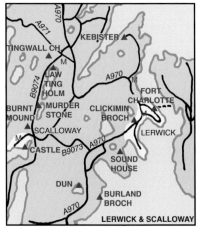

LERWICK & SCALLOWAY

castle (HU404392) is almost surrounded by modern buildings around the small but busy harbour. Scalloway has a small museum. After visiting Scalloway, take the B9074 road towards Tingwall. Just as this road leaves the main A970, a large burnt mound stands to the W of the road (80). On the hilltop behind is a large modern house, during construction of which, in the early 1990s, a broch and a medieval cemetery were discovered and excavated. Heading N along the valley, the bright grass and ruined limekilns indicate that this is limestone, and some of Shetland's most fertile land. On the right, the Murder Stone (61) lies close beside the road, while 2km further on, loch-side parking allows a good view of the Law Ting Holm (128), site of

Shetland's late Norse legislative assembly. The church of Tingwall (HU419438) to the N of the loch is on a very old site, and was almost certainly the principal church of Shetland in late medieval times. A medieval vault with some interesting gravestones survives.

Turn right at the Tingwall crossroads and climb the hill to rejoin the A970, following this back towards Lerwick. At the foot of the hill just N of the town, before the power station, stands the Bod of Gremista (HU464432). This is an old trading place and house, now restored as a small museum. A side road to the left leads out past industrial sites and ends at Kebister (118), where the visible remains of a late medieval teind (tithe) barn overlie a complex of remains dating back into the Iron Age. This is the northern element in a string of sites running up the limestone-rich Tingwall valley, which can fairly be said to be the heart of medieval Shetland.

Returning to Lerwick, time should be taken to visit Fort Charlotte, an early-modern artillery fort built to counter the threat of French raids. It gives a fine view of the north harbour area, including the old warehouse buildings at Hay's Dock, now converted to provide Shetland's new Museum, Gallery and Archives.

CUNNINGSBURGH and MOUSA

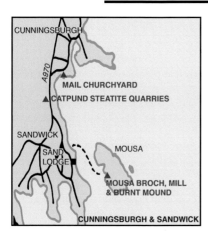

CUNNINGSBURGH & SANDWICK

Starting point: at South Brig of Cunningsburgh (HU428281). Note the churchyard of Mail to the E, above the shore, site of the recent find of a Pictish carved stone (HU433279). Drive S on the A970 and turn onto a cut-off road loop on the right, which allows parking by the stile giving access to Burn of Catpund, the finest quarried steatite outcrop in Shetland (129). Traces of the carving of bowls can be seen in the bed and sides of the burn.

Continue S, turning off to Sand Lodge (HU436249) signposted for the island of Mousa, site of the famous broch (105). A boat runs scheduled trips in summer from Sand Lodge pier (see gazetteer entry for Mousa broch). On the island, the landing place is beside a small shepherd's hut, and the path leads S over the shoulder of the hill, giving a fine view of the broch and, behind it, the ruined laird's house or "haa". A ruined mill is passed beside a small stream en route for the broch, and a small burnt mound lies further up this stream.

There are some interesting abandoned crofts on the island, which is also famous for its wildlife. Seals breed at the south end of the island. It also supports many seabirds, most notably stormy petrels which nest in the shingle beach beside the broch. The walls above the boat-landing are one of the best places to see the local Shetland race of the common wren, distinguished by richer brown colouring and slightly larger size from its Scottish cousin – the high-pitched song is surprisingly powerful for such a small bird, and the local family seems to have become accustomed to visitors.

LEVENWICK, BODDAM and BIGTON

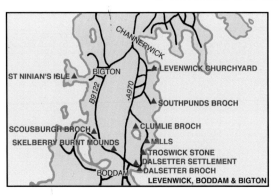

LEVENWICK, BODDAM & BIGTON

Starting point: Levenwick cemetery (HU414213). The graveyard is set on a large mound suggesting either many centuries of burials or perhaps something else – maybe a broch – underneath. A 1.5km walk from here S along the high ground overlooking the coast leads to the broch of Southpunds (HU415197), excavated over a century ago and now badly dilapidated: a terrible warning of the dangers of excavating sites with no thought about their future care. The site was a complex one, with many similarities to Clickimin. It is possible to use minor roads to find a shorter access route.

Back in the car, head S and take the road to Clumlie (106). The broch here is set in the middle of a deserted croft, with the house and outbuildings constructed around a large stony mound which was only later revealed to be a broch. The place name Clumlie has been suggested by some as deriving from Columb-chille, the Gaelic name for Columba. If so, this would make it virtually the only Gaelic-derived name in Shetland. Continuing S on the minor road there is a fine group of small "Norse" mills on the burn which comes out of Loch of Clumlie, and between the road and the loch are the

remains of a sluice (HU404173). On the S side of the valley of this burn, overlooking the croft of Troswick (= trolls' bay) is a fine standing stone (66).

Continuing S, the site of the broch at Dalsetter (107) with its outer ramparts forms a prominent feature on the E of the road. Between the broch and the road is a prehistoric settlement (24) with the remains of three small houses, field walls and clearance cairns. Follow the road onwards to Boddam, passing an interesting 18th-century merchant's house with upper floor store, accessed by an external stair (HU398155).

Rejoin the main road and almost immediately leave it again, following signs for Bigton on the B9122. On the right (N) are the Skelberry burnt mounds (83), in a typical streamside location. Further on, buildings near a small garage on the left of the road cluster around a large mound, which contains the broch of Scousburgh (HU377178). The road now turns N, with views across typical small farms and crofts, showing remnants of the old strip-fields. On a clear day, the hilly profile of the outlying island of Foula can be seen to the W. The cliffs at the Kame of Foula are among the tallest sheer cliffs in Great Britain.

Turn left and follow signs to St Ninian's Isle, parking and then walking across the remarkable beach to the chapel site (121). Bird watchers may find breeding puffins onshore on the W side of the Isle during the breeding season, though numbers are much reduced. The B9122 through Bigton leads back up to the main A970 road at Channerwick (HU398155) where some of the steepest fields in Shetland, now abandoned, were once cultivated by hard-working crofters.

*SUMBURGH

Starting point: Sumburgh House Hotel (HU400096). Park in the bays marked for Jarlshof, and walk down to the site (25). This is probably the longest-lived settlement site so far excavated in Scotland, with a start in the Bronze Age and an end in the 17th century AD. Overlooking the site of Jarlshof is Sumburgh Head, reached by a minor road. Park before the gates of the wall around the lighthouse buildings. As the road passes through the wall, it also passes across the ditches of an Iron Age fort, now largely concealed by modern foundations. This was presumably Swein's fort, from which the name Sumburgh is thought to derive.

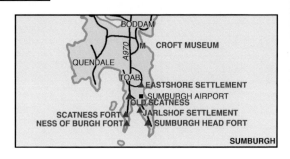

Back on the main road, pass the access for Jarlshof and continue to the junction for Scatness, and turn down it to the S. Park at the road end and walk along a track and then over short grass towards the promontory forts of Scatness North (109) and then onwards to Ness of Burgi (110), taking care on the rocky slope above the short strip of shingle beach. The latter is the classic Shetland blockhouse fort, and was excavated in the 1930s and is now consolidated. Scatness North, although more eroded, was very similar – it was excavated in the early 1980s but has not been consolidated, because marine erosion was too far advanced. This pair of forts could be interpreted as lookout posts or as bridgeheads, set on the most southerly practical landing points. But why two so close together?

Return to the car, and proceed back to the main road and N towards Lerwick. After only a few yards, park on the left overlooking the sea and the S side of the end of the airport's main runway. On the right (cross the road with care) is the

important Iron Age and Pictish period site of Old Scatness, excavated from 1995 onwards. The complex of stone buildings clustered around the lower levels of a broch represents the most extensive Iron Age settlement so far found in Shetland. The post-excavation consolidation of the site, plus some smaller-scale research, is still under way at time of writing, but there will be on-site visitor information with various activities during the summer months. (See gazetteer entry for contact information.)

Proceeding N on the A970, notice beyond the low modern building of the boat club, a headland on the N side of the tidal Pool of Virkie which is crowned by a small ruined house. This is a site called Eastshore (HU403113). So far unexcavated, it may have the same range of dates as Jarlshof, containing at least a broch (half eroded by the sea), Norse houses and medieval farm remains, as well as the more recent croft buildings. Late Neolithic finds have been made from the eroding shoreline. Clearly the S end of Shetland is rich in major sites – perhaps because of the easily cultivated sandy soil combined with its strategic position.

Continue N on the A970 over the hill, then turn right to Southvoe, to visit the Shetland Croft House museum, a fine

Tours

refurbished croft complex, with nearby a reconstructed working example of a "Norse" mill (HU398146). Although not

an ancient building, its style and furnishings reflect traditions reaching back at least a thousand years.

*BRESSAY

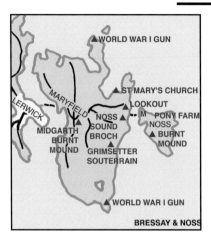

AWORLD WAR I GUN

AST MARY'S CHURCH
ALOOKOUT
M PONY FARM
NOSS A
NOSS
SOUND
BURNT
BROCH A BURNT
MOUND
GRIMSETTER
SOUTERRAIN
LERWICK
MARYFIELD
MIDGARTH
BURNT
MOUND

A WORLD WAR I GUN

BRESSAY & NOSS

Starting point: Bressay Ferry terminal, Lerwick Harbour. Take the regular vehicle ferry across to Maryfield on Bressay. Follow the road up to a T-junction, and then turn right (following signs towards Noss) and left past the church in the small village, climbing up into the centre of the island. After the road levels out at the top of the hill, follow the left branch to Setter, park where the road becomes a rough track and continue on foot to the broch and chapel site at Cullingsburgh (119) – one of Shetland's finest Pictish carved stones came from here. There is a burnt mound just before the churchyard is reached.

A track diverging N from the Setter road allows a diversion to Aith and on to Score Head (HU513447), which has the remains of World War One coastal defences, including a large gun and the remains of the camp which housed the small garrison. (A similar site, also with a gun, exists at the S end of Bressay (HU516357), but this is a rather longer walk.) The lookout tower on the hilltop

(HU524415) towards the E side of the island is also a wartime structure.

Return along the Setter road to the junction and turn sharply left, towards Noss. Park at the road end and take the steep path down towards the shore, passing the remains of Noss Sound broch (103). During the summer, a small ferry carries visitors across to Noss, which is a Nature Reserve managed by Scottish Natural Heritage for its seabird interests. There is not much visible archaeology on Noss, except the very slight traces of a chapel just S of the warden's house (HU531410) and an unimpressive burnt mound on the SW shore of the island (HU539401). The main feature of historic interest is the (restored) stable complex beside the boat landing at Gungstie (HU531411), recalling the days in the early 19th century when the island was used for breeding ponies to be used in the coalfields of Scotland and England.

Return to Bressay and follow the outward road back to the shore. A detour along a track leading off to the S (left) just past a small loch leads for 1.5km to the old croft at Wadbister, where with some searching a small souterrain can be found to the S of Loch of Grimsetter (112). Back on the "main" road, continue towards the W, noting a fine burnt mound on the left at Midgarth, halfway down the hill towards the village (HU499408). Once the W shore is reached near the church, a branch to the S leads to the old lighthouse buildings, beyond which a 3km walk leads along spectacular cliffs, past the old croft of Dale and out to the S end of the island at Bard Head. Return to the ferry and Lerwick.

WHITENESS, WEISDALE and NESTING

Starting point: junction of the A971 and the road for South Whiteness, beside the old school (HU392467). A burnt mound stands a short distance to the S of the starting point. To the NE, in Loch of Strom, stand the remains of a small, early, stone castle, probably dating to the days of the Sinclair Earls in the 14th or early 15th century (HU395476). There is a causeway from the nearby shore, which gives access at low tide (the brackish loch is slightly affected by tides). Continue N on the A971, passing a jewellery workshop on the right – which bases some of its designs on archaeological artefacts. A short distance onwards, on the left hand side, there is a fine burnt mound (HU389477), and it is possible to walk round the head of the bay to the prehistoric homestead at Olligarth (HU 388473). This can be seen clearly from the road as a greener area of ground surrounded by a tumbled stone wall.

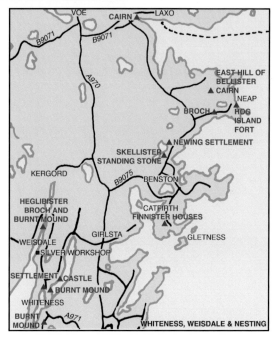

Following the road N past Whiteness School and a cluster of modern houses, there is a good view across the Weisdale Voe to Sound (HU383501), with its ruined laird's house, chapel, graveyard and small harbour. Along the hillside to the N, and a little higher up, the obvious green mound beside a house called Heglibister may conceal a cairn or a broch, while down-slope from it another burnt mound lies near to the water.

From the head of Weisdale Voe, take the B9075 road, through the trees at Kergord (HU395542) and on into the heart of Mainland, joining the A970 main road, which runs N-S along the spine of the island, at Lamba Scord. Take the road S for 2km then turn left towards Nesting, passing through Catfirth. Turn right towards Benston and then take a right fork towards Gletness, climbing up onto higher ground. As this road begins to fall

towards the houses by the shore, park and walk SW past the abandoned croft of Finnister to two prehistoric houses (12). The whole of South Nesting is rich in interesting humps and bumps, some archaeological sites and some the result of limestone quarrying.

Retrace the road back to the fork, and then drive N through Garth and past Skellister, parking where the minor road rejoins the B9075. The prominent standing stone called the "Auld Wife" (52) overlooks the area from the hillside above the road. Turning N, the B9075 passes through the group of prehistoric houses at Newing (11). One house lies to the left of the road, two close by on the right and one further down the slope on the right, near the sea. At the junction by the memorial at Brettabister, turn right. Pass Housabister, where the scattered foundations of a broch can be found just

Tours

behind the chapel (HU487578), and proceed to Neap, at the end of the road. From here it is a short walk ESE downhill to Hog Island Sound fort (99). The chambered cairn of East Hill of Bellister (51) lies partway up the SE slope of the tall hill to the W of Neap.

Back on the road, return to the junction and turn right, heading NW towards Laxo (the name means "salmon river", and the stream has a fine waterfall, especially when in spate). A rather featureless mound beyond the burn may be a ruined cairn or else a

burnt mound with some unusually large stones in its makeup (HU445635). At the junction nearby, a right turn leads to the ferry for Whalsay, but to complete this tour turn left and drive W to Voe, a pleasant cluster of houses at the head of Olna Firth, with a slightly Norwegian appearance. In times gone past, before the modern road network was established, the narrow neck of land between Laxo and Voe served as a shortcut for many travelling E-W, saving them a long boat trip round the N or S of Mainland.

*WEST MAINLAND 1

Starting point: A971 road beside the shop at Bixter (HU332523). Take the B9071, signed for Aith, soon branching left towards Clousta. As the first houses of Clousta appear, after about 4km, a small prehistoric house with a surrounding field wall lies on the left: the road actually cuts the field wall (HU314569).

Continue to the road end at Noonsbrough, noting a good burnt mound just across the fence on the left (75). From the road end, take the track SW over the hill and down to near the shore at Point of Hurds, where in a small valley (HU289568) lies a small prehistoric house and a mound, which

may be another house or else a large cairn, plus a few field clearance heaps. Walk N from here, keeping well up the hillside until the ridge falls away, and drop down to the NW past the remains of a chambered cairn on a shoulder to reach the little loch on the neck of land before Longa Ness. Here an oval prehistoric house lies below a stone-built sheep shelter, with a second house about 100m to the E of it. Around these are the remains of an extensive field system, including some quite sizeable clearance cairns.

Climb back up the hill to the E, North Ward of Noonsbrough, on whose summit is a much modified chambered cairn (54) and then head SE, dropping quickly. There is a good view from above of the remains of Noonsbrough broch (HU295576), which stands on a small island that is now linked to the shore by two shingle beaches. The broch is largely concealed by the walls of more recent buildings.

Rejoin the road and return to Bixter. Those on foot may take a diversion across the moor from Greenmeadow, past a standing stone (HU325558) to pick up the Aith road again at Harwell, and thus to Aith or Bixter.

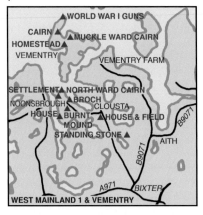

WEST MAINLAND 1 & VEMENTRY

*VEMENTRY

Those wishing to visit this interesting island should make enquiries at the Tourist Office in Lerwick about boat hire.

Starting point: road end at Vementry farm (HU308597). From the boat landing head NW towards the highest hill, the Muckle Ward, which is crowned by the best preserved chambered cairn in Shetland (53). To the SW of the summit, at the head of Northra Voe, is a ruined prehistoric homestead (HU293608) and to the NW of this, at the foot of a hill slope, is a ruined cairn (HU289612).

Having come this far, only the most resolutely prehistoric-minded would miss the chance to visit the nearby headland of Swarbacks Head, where two large guns and the command post survive from a First World War coastal defence battery which protected the approach to Swarbacks Minn, which served as the forward base for a cruiser squadron. The guns here and on Bressay (see above) are among the youngest "ancient monuments" in Scotland, dating from 1918 and given legal protection in 1992. Retired from their original role as the primary armament of a heavy warship, the guns were put in place by being winched up the cliffs from the deck of a naval supply ship anchored as close inshore as was possible. Their survival is due to the inaccessibility of their location relative to their value as scrap metal.

Return to the pre-arranged boat pick-up.

WEST MAINLAND 2

Starting point: at the road junction between the A971 and the B9071 at Park Hall (HU313527). The chambered cairn of Ara Clett (59) lies on top of the small hill behind the large house (Park Hall) to the N of the road. Take the B9071 SE then S past Garderhouse. To the SE, where Seli Voe reaches the sea, note the island of Kirk Holm. This has the remains of a possible monastic site at its N end (127, see gazetteer for route allowing a closer view).

The B9071 rises to cross high ground before dropping into Easter Skeld, which is overlooked from the W by a chambered cairn (HU305450). Further S, most easily reached off the minor road which runs S from the head of the bay at Easter Skeld, is a fine standing stone (60). The chambered cairn is most easily reached from the highest point of the B9071 road once past the township.

Back on the road, continue W, then take the minor road to the right signed

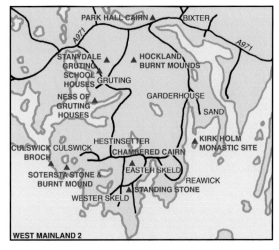

WEST MAINLAND 2

for Culswick (HU272450). Park and take the track uphill past a small chapel. Follow a convenient but not beautiful bulldozed track round the N side of Loch of Sotersta. As this track nears the sea, there is an excellent view across a small loch towards the broch of Culswick

(102). A recently constructed stone causeway leads across the N end of the loch in the direction of the broch, which is one of the tallest unexcavated brochs in Shetland. It is built of red granite, with a striking triangular lintel over its entrance.

To return, head S from the broch and then E to cross the S end of the loch, continuing in this direction over a slight riser to the deserted croft of Sotersta (HU262446) where a standing stone has been incorporated into the corner of a now-ruined outhouse. A small burnt mound lies beside the nearby stream. Head NE along a rough track back to the chapel and back down to the road.

Retrace the minor road back to the B9071, and 1km E of the junction, head N on another minor road at Hestinsetter, passing Olas Voe and (another) Seli Voe to reach the crossroads at Gruting (HU286495). Taking the left-hand road to its end, park and walk S to the prehistoric settlement at Ness of Gruting

(20). Back at the Gruting crossroads, the central road leads NW to the prehistoric houses at Gruting School (19). But if time is running short, the essential visit is to Stanydale, so take the right-hand road, and after about 1km park at the Historic Scotland roadside sign. From here it is a gentle, though sometimes rather damp, 700m across grassy moorland, way-marked by posts, to the remarkable "temple" or hall of Stanydale (18) with its attendant upright stones and remains of houses and fields. One of these houses was excavated at the same time as the "temple", in the 1940s, and its foundations lie beside one of the marker posts. Stanydale lies in a shallow basin, and several of the low hills surrounding it bear ruined cairns.

Return to the road by the outward route, and drive N, passing the burnt mounds at Hockland (77) on the right, just below a croft, to regain the A971 at the starting point.

WEST MAINLAND 3

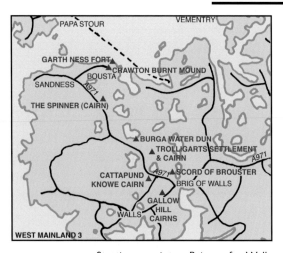

settlements of Pinhoulland and then, over a rise to the SW, Loch of Grunnavoe.

For the purpose of the present tour, however, take the branch signed for Sandness and stop before the top of the first hill in lay-by to visit the excavated and now backfilled prehistoric settlement of Scord of Brouster (15). A good view is obtained from the information board on the slope overlooking the houses. Further along the road, at the junction with the back road to Walls, is the very ruined possible long cairn of Cattapund Knowe (57) – this requires the eye of faith to discern much among a tumble of much rebuilt stone. 1km further along the Sandness road, the area to the right is Trolligarts (14) (just to the E of the chambered cairn marked on the OS map), a complex of house foundations,

Starting point: Brig of Walls (HU260512), where the A971 splits into two. Walking S along the W shore of the inlet, Voe of Browland, leads to the field walls and clearance cairns. The houses are obscured by later sheep pens and cabbage patches, and the whole area "feels" as if much more might be identified by careful survey. Trolligarts (pronounced "trowie yirts") means "trolls' yards". Neither of the cairns marked on the map is particularly impressive.

Continuing NW on the A971, there is a good view of Burga Water's dun (101) – a ruined, lightweight broch – to the right. The road twists through peaty moorland before beginning to drop towards the fertile area of Sandness. On the right, at the top of the hill, is the large cairn called The Spinner (55).

Take the right-hand minor road towards Bousta, stopping in a dip just before a public telephone kiosk. A gate on the N side of the road gives access to a track, and a splendid burnt mound – one of Shetland's shapeliest, stands on the left of the track, not far from the road (74). Follow the track onwards past some ruined mills before diverging to the N just before an uninhabited croft to reach the shore at Garth, where a short scramble over a rocky beach and up a steep slope leads to Ness of Garth (100), a promontory fort with remains of stone walls on the landward side and traces of several small houses within, which may be later houses, perhaps hinting at an early monastic presence on this site.

Back on the road, return to the A971 and back to Cattapund Knowe, turning right towards the village of Walls (HU245495), once a thriving herring port and still interestingly littered with the remains of piers, wharves and a ruined fish-oil plant. Return in the direction of Lerwick, passing two large cairns on the left at the foot of Gallow Hill (58) just before reaching Brig of Walls.

*HILLSWICK & ESHANESS

Starting point: the public parking area at the seafront in Hillswick (HU282750). Follow the narrow public road SSW to its end at Findlins, then head SW over rising ground to the prehistoric house at Grevasand (7), which sits high up on exposed grassland, near spectacular cliffs. There is a steatite outcrop on the cliffs to the W, but do not approach too closely! From the house site, head SE to a small loch at Niddister, with a substantial burnt mound situated at its nearest end (72). Return to Hillswick, either due N of by heading E to reach the shore and following this back.

From Hillswick take the A970 and then the B9078 road for Esha Ness. At Burnside (70) is a fine burnt mound, clearly visible from the road, and after passing the small prehistoric house immediately N of the road at Black Water (6) take the right fork signed for Esha Ness lighthouse. (The main road heads left, and leads after a short distance to Stenness, a beautiful bay with the remains of a 19th century fishing station, at HU215772.)

Heading towards the lighthouse, a small loch on the left has another good burnt mound (71) beside it at the end nearest the road, and is overlooked by the ruined church and graveyard of Cross Kirk. Follow the road almost to the

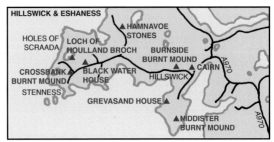

145

lighthouse, park and then strike NNE across short cliff-top grassland to reach the broch at Loch of Houlland, which forms a very impressive mound in the shallow loch – surely its site was chosen for dramatic effect rather than defence, as the loch is very shallow. There are ruined "Norse" mills beside the little

stream, which drains the loch and falls into a collapsed cave, the Holes of Scraada (HU213793). The cliffs here are very spectacular, composed of ancient volcanic rocks, and a good watching point for puffins during the nesting season.

Return to the lighthouse, skirting the heads of the long inlets, or "geos".

NORTH ROE

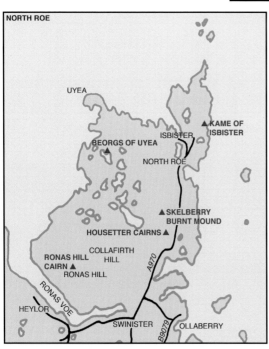

(Fethaland on OS map) (HU374942) about 3.5km N along a well-surfaced track – a splendid walk on a good day.)

Drive S on the A970 to North Roe, parking near the school (HU364896). Take a recently upgraded, but still rather rough, track for a long walk W to reach the N-facing slope above Mill Loch, the Beorgs of Uyea, where there are many scattered traces of ancient stone-quarrying for polished stone implement manufacture and one particularly fine working site (5). Back on the road, follow the A970 S past the burnt mound at Skelberry (HU365869) to Housetter, where there are remains of three chambered cairns, two near the road and one high up on the hillside (43). One of the cairns is reduced to a low mound of rubble with just two large blocks left upright. These once framed the ends of the cairn's façade.

S again, passing the Brig of Collafirth – where very slight remains from a 19th century whaling station survive – a deteriorating access road on the W side leads up to the old radio station on Collafirth Hill. Park near this untidy and windswept monument to communications technology, and then head W to climb Ronas Hill. This is Shetland's highest point, and is crowned by a chambered cairn (44) which is in remarkable repair but has probably been re-roofed and certainly modified since the Neolithic. This is a splendid walk in

Starting point: the very N end of the public road at Isbister (HU371909). Head E up a small burn to a loch, and then follow the top of the cliffs N to obtain a good view of the setting of the monastic settlement on the exposed Kame of Isbister (116), although the building foundations are on the seaward side and cannot be seen from the shore. Return to the road-end. (There is an interesting 19th century fishing station in a beautiful location at Fedaland fine weather, offering a chance of sweeping views and an experience of sub-arctic vegetation and landforms, but in poor weather only the most dedicated Neolithic enthusiast will find it rewarding!

The tour may be extended by taking the road that runs along the S shore of Ronas Voe as far as Heylor (HU292810), where the ruined pier marks where whales were once brought ashore to be "processed" into their useful components. Heylor is the only one, out of at least four such locations in Shetland, where anything significant survives of structures associated with a brief phase of "industrial" offshore whaling in the early 19th century. From just E of Heylor, a road cuts over the hill to rejoin the main Hillswick to Lerwick road at Urafirth.

*WHALSAY

Starting point: the ferry terminal at Symbister (HU537625). Around the bay to the NE are the remains of 16th and 17th century Hanseatic merchants' houses, one of which, the "Bremen Booth" has been restored (HU539625). Continue along this road for 3km to an old quarry beside the road at Muckle Breck (HU586681). Park here and head S to reach the excavated prehistoric houses of the Yoxie Stones (3) and the Benie Hoose (2). The foundations of a miniature cairn on Pettigarths Field (39) overlook them from the N. Return to the road. There is a standing stone further to the NE, at Skaw (38).

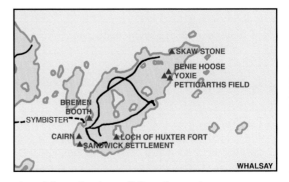

Backtrack to Brough and then take the road which goes SE to Isbister, following the road as it turns SE towards Huxter, where a small Iron Age fort sits on a small island (96) off the S shore of the loch. It is accessible (just) via a rather perilous semi-submerged causeway, but is as well viewed from the shore. Follow the road onwards and then take a left fork down to Sandwick (HU543617). Park on the road and walk down to the bay on the SE, where may be found the remains of four prehistoric houses and two burnt mounds (4).

Return to the ferry terminal, if time permits climbing the small hill to its SW, which has a ruined chambered cairn (41) on its summit and a fine view.

*FETLAR

Starting point: ferry terminal at Oddsta (HU582942).

Drive 1km S, park by the road and head due W to the shore, where there are the remains of a rapidly eroding Iron Age site, probably a fort rather than a broch, despite the name, Snabrough (95). Back on the road, follow it S to Brough Lodge, where the squat round tower of the 19th century buildings to the W is situated on the foundations of a broch. Turn left for Tresta, where the site of Papil, and early Christian chapel, lies beside a very fine sandy beach (HU604903).

Further along the road, as it begins to

147

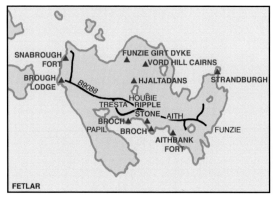

FETLAR

Turn onto a minor road at Funzie, which runs N for 2km to Everland. Park here and walk a further 2km N to reach the monastic site of Strandburgh (125). Return by the same route, and then back along the road to the ferry.

(This extension is on the RSPB-managed Nature Reserve and must not be visited from March until mid-August without permission from the locally based Warden – see individual gazetteer entries for contact details.) From the road at HU617912, turn up this and park beside the airstrip. Walk due N to Hjaltadans (36) and on to Vord Hill, which has two cairns on its flat summit (HU622936). On the N and W flanks of Vord Hill, the Funzie Girt (1) is a massive boundary wall of prehistoric date. From here, return to the airstrip, either direct or via the next hill to the SW, Stackaberg (HU613928), which is crowned by what the OS map calls a cairn but which may be an unusually-sited prehistoric settlement site, perhaps of Bronze Age or Iron Age date – rabbit scrapes in its surface have produced pottery sherds which would fit this period.

fall towards the next bay, park and walk S to the broch of Houbie (94) with its surrounding ditch and banks. The coastline at the head of the bay is disfigured with the abandoned remains of quarrying of steatite, which was crushed to produce talc. Some older workings, probably medieval, survive SW of the broch. Back on the road, continue SE past the Ripple Stone (37) and the remains of a broch at Aith (HU629901). Beyond the bay, the Wick of Aith, there is a small multiple-banked promontory fort (95).

SOUTH & MID YELL

Starting point: the ferry terminal at Ulsta (HU453795). As the ferry completes its crossing towards Yell, the small island on the right, close in to the Yell shore, is Holm of Copister, which is almost entirely occupied by a ruined broch with outer walls. On landing, take the B9081 E towards Burravoe, passing the burnt mound at Kettlester (67). The Old Haa at Burravoe has been converted into a small visitor centre.

N on the B9081 road signed for Mid Yell, after 3.5km a side-road on the right leads to Gossabrough. The broch mound here (124) is flanked by traces of very old rectilinear houses, possibly of late Norse

date. Back on the B9081, continue N until the branch for Aywick, and take the more northerly of two roads which head E towards the shore. 1km ENE beyond the end of this road is the site at Stoal (92), once described as a broch but almost certainly a small multiple-banked promontory fort.

Proceed to Mid Yell (HU507908) and turn left onto the main road back towards Ulsta. Not far along the road, at the head of the long inlet of Whale Firth, a ruined laird's house high on the N side of the road lies beside the remains of a broch. On the slope behind it, not far above the shore, is a small heel-shaped cairn (35). Unusually built into the slope of the hill, it now survives as little more than the façade.

3km further S and W along the road, just as the houses of West Sandwick come into view on the right, a peat track heads off to the right. A walk along this, past Ladie Loch and Mill Loch to the Loch of Birriesgirt, reaches the coast just S of the almost inaccessible monastic site of Birrier of West Sandwick (115). Return to the road and onwards to Ulsta, passing high above Head of Brough (HU445849), where there is another very ruined broch.

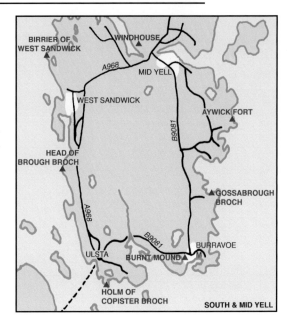

NORTH YELL

Starting point: the ferry terminal at Gutcher (HU548993). Take the main road SW for a short distance, then turn off left towards North Sandwick, passing a standing stone on the left (33) to park at the end of the road. Walk S to the bay, then, climbing to skirt above low cliffs, out to Burra Ness. The broch (91) is clearly visible on the headland, and is flanked by much-reduced ramparts and traces of old fields. A number of boat nousts (hollows to protect boats from the elements) may be seen along the shore W of the broch, while a probable burial cairn, perhaps of Bronze Age date, is located about 400m SW of the broch (HU553953). If visiting in the early morning or at dusk, this is one of the best otter-spotting places in the islands.

Returning to the car, drive N to join the B9082 which continues N past Gutcher and Cullivoe to the North Yell School, where a minor road leads E to

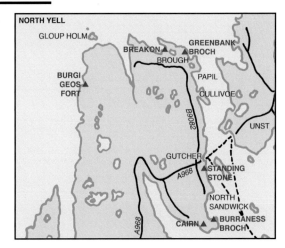

the chapel site of Papil (HP543041), where little but the placename survives. About 500m further along the B9082, NE of Brough, a large green mound represents the broch at Greenbank (HP539051), from which stretches for 1.5km to the W the sandy area of

Breakon (32), which has revealed ruins and artefacts of many periods as the sand dunes have shifted over the centuries, and doubtless has more to reveal. (High up on the edge of the dunes a 17th century house, now in ruins, incorporates fragments of Dutch yellow brick, probably brought to Shetland as ballast by fishing or trading boats hoping to return with cargoes of local fish.)

Back on the B9082, follow this road and its unclassified extension to the road end at Gloup (HU507046). The small island visible to the NW is Gloup Holm (HP486062), where many years ago digging revealed traces of what may have been a ruined broch in this very exposed but strategic location. From Gloup a track leads S, past the memorial to the great fishing disaster at the end of the 19th century – remains of the fishing station lie beside the water at the foot of the hill. A long and lonely walk leads along this track to the head of Gloup Voe, then W up the valley of Rules Gill and over the moor to descend to the W side of Yell at the spectacular promontory fort at Burgi Geos (90). Return by the same route, and so back to Gutcher.

*SOUTH & WEST UNST

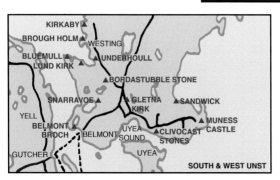

SOUTH & WEST UNST

Starting point: the ferry terminal at Belmont (HP565005). Walk NW round the bay to the broch at Hoga Ness (89), which has a fine set of ramparts. Back at the car, drive N along the A968 road, noticing on the left the abandoned crofts and the small lynchetted fields of the former township of Snarravoe (HP572023). Turn onto the B9084 through Uyeasound and, climbing out of Uyeasound, pass on the right the standing stones at Clivocast (31) before the road runs on to Muness Castle (HP629012), built in the last years of the 16th century. Heading back towards Uyeasound, take the right-hand road out to Hannigarth and from here walk gently downhill to reach the S end of the bay of Sand Wick (123) where there are the remains of a late Norse house excavated in the 1980s and a low, rectangular, Pictish period burial cairn.

Return down to Uyeasound, taking the first road on the right at the head of the bay up past Gletna Kirk (HP592020). This very ruined chapel has an obscure history, but was for many years regarded as a healing site. Rejoin the A968 but soon branch W onto the road signed for Westing. The name of the W side of the island derives from Unst having once been divided into several local assemblies, or "things", and is locally still "The Westing" – the west thing, which is a survival of an old usage. In most cases, "The" (or "Da" in Shetland speech) has been dropped in, for example Nesting (the thing of the headlands) or Delting (the thing of the valley). After about 1km, a road on the right heads off past the large standing stone at Bordastubble (30), offering a diversion past the old House of Lund to a ruined church and graveyard, beyond which it is a short walk to the monastic settlement on the headland called Blue Mull (114).

Back on the Westing road, one soon passes, on the left, the large mound of Underhoull broch (88) and its surrounding ramparts. Just down the slope below the broch are the remains of Norse houses excavated many years ago, which were found to overlie Pictish period and Iron Age dwellings. The public road ends on the shore of a shingly bay with a small island, Brough Holm, which bears another broch, now rapidly eroding (HP566058). Walk N around the bay to the next headland, where on a small knoll a modern building sits on top of an early chapel site at Kirkaby (HP566065). Return to the main road and turn S to the ferry or N to commence the next tour.

*NORTH & EAST UNST

Starting point: the junction of the main A968 and the Westing road (HP591029). 2km N along the A968 the ruined cairn of Watlee (28) lies just W of the road, while 2km further again the two cairns of Hill of Caldback (29) lie to the E. Descending into Baltasound, the main road goes right at a crossroads, but go straight ahead, leaving the old chapel on the right-hand side. When a T-junction is reached, turn right and park as soon as is safe. From here, climb due N up Crussa Field, encountering just before its summit the three Rounds of Tivla (27). There are also two cairns on the very summit. In good weather, it is a pleasant walk E along the ridge to the cairns on Muckle Heog (26).

The notably rusty colouring of the rocks in this area of Unst is a result of unusual mineralogy, derived from their origin as part of the Earth's crust deep below the floor of an ancient ocean. Ores of chromium and other metals were once mined in Unst, as was talc. The piers from which these minerals were shipped until recently can be seen at Baltasound (HP633091), and the Shetland Museum holds some excellent specimens.

Back at the car, drive into Baltasound, on the N side of the inlet of the same name. On the long narrow island of Balta, which almost closes the mouth of the bay, a broch ruin set on a low cliff looks eastwards out to sea (HP660089).

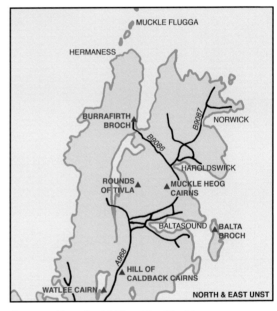

Continue N on the A968 to Haroldswick and then NW on the B9086 to Burrafirth, where another ruined broch stands just S of the shore station for the now-automated Muckle Flugga lighthouse, overshadowed from the hilltop opposite by the aerials of RAF Saxa Vord, itself now redundant. From Burrafirth a path runs N through a nature reserve to Herma Ness (HP605183), from which can be seen Muckle Flugga, white with gannets and their nests, and Out Stack (HP612202), the most northerly point of the British

Isles. Return to Haroldswick. Before heading S take the time to visit the Unst Boat Haven, a fine collection of traditional small sailing vessels.

Local contacts & useful information

Sites and monuments

If you think you have discovered an unrecorded site, take a note of its location or grid reference as exactly as you can, take a photograph or two if possible, then check with the Shetland Amenity Trust's archaeology staff. The Trust maintains the Shetland Sites and Monuments Record – which is held on computer and is likely to become accessible on-line during the currency of this edition – and can quickly establish if your discovery is already recorded or not, and follow it up if necessary. The Trust can also provide information on archaeological issues ranging from old excavations to requirements for developers.

Shetland Archaeologist
Shetland Amenity Trust
Garthspool, Lerwick
ZE1 0NY
01595 694688
shetamenity.trust@zetnet.co.uk

Artefacts and finds

If you find an artefact, such as a carved stone or some ancient pottery, it is best to leave it in place and inform the proper authority – a guideline that even professional archaeologists have been known to ignore! The reason for this advice is that an artefact on the surface may be protruding from a whole archaeological site below. If the artefact is completely free of the ground, or so small it might become lost before a return visit, mark the find-spot clearly on the ground and the location on a map, and contact the Shetland Museum. The museum has an excellent collection of past discoveries, including artefacts from many digs. It also has an excellent display of more recent artefacts, which provide insights into Shetland life stretching back into prehistoric times, and a splendid collection of old photographs.

From 2006, in new premises at:
Shetland Museum
Hay's Dock
Lerwick
museum@sic.shetland.gov.uk

Either / or ?

Not sure which? There is some overlap between responsibilities. If you find an archaeological site which has artefacts eroding out of it, perhaps pottery or large amounts of old bones, it is best to contact the Archaeologist, because the needs of the site will need to be addressed, not just the objects. But don't worry – the Museum and the Archaeologist work closely together.

Legalities

All ancient objects found in Scotland (not just obviously precious items) must be reported for possible Treasure Trove Action: the Museum is the place to report. In law, finders are not keepers, and landowners in Scotland have no rights of ownership over ancient objects found on their land.

There is no legal requirement to report newly discovered sites, but it is recommended: this keeps records up to date and avoids the risk of a site being destroyed because nobody else knows it exists. Over 200 of the most important sites in Shetland are legally protected against damage or disturbance as scheduled ancient monuments. You can check if a site is protected on-line at:
http://www.historic-scotland.gov.uk/index/ancientmonuments

Historic Scotland
Inspectorate
Longmore House
Salisbury Place
Edinburgh
EH9 1SH
0131 668 8766 – ask for "scheduled monuments general enquiries"

Further reading

Ashmore, P.J. *Jarlshof*, Edinburgh, 2003. (Historic Scotland guide.)

Berry, R.J. and Johnston, J.L. *The Natural History of Shetland*, London, 1980.

Crawford, B.E. (ed) *Essays in Shetland History*, Lerwick, 1984.

Fenton, A. and Palsson, H. (eds) *The Northern and Western Isles in the Viking World*, Edinburgh, 1984.

Fojut, N. and Pringle, R.D. *The Ancient Monuments of Shetland*, Edinburgh, 1992. (Historic Scotland guide – covers Stanydale, Mousa, Clickimin, Ness of Burgi.)

Graham-Campbell, G. and Batey, C.E. *Vikings in Scotland: an Archaeological Survey*, Edinburgh, 1998.

Ritchie, A. *Exploring Scotland's Heritage: Shetland*, Edinburgh, 1996.

Schei, L.K. and Moberg, G. *The Shetland Story*, London, 1988.

Stewart, J. *Shetland Place-names*, Lerwick, 1987.

Turner, V. *Ancient Shetland*, London, 1998.

Turner, V. *How to be a detective*, Lerwick 1991. (Children's book.)

Turner V. *The Shaping of Shetland: Developments in Shetland Landscape Archaeology*, Lerwick, 1998.

Maps

Ordnance Survey 1:50000 Landranger
Sheet 1   Shetland, Yell, Unst & Fetlar
Sheet 2 Shetland, Sullom Voe & Whalsay
Sheet 3   Shetland, North Mainland
Sheet 4   Shetland, South Mainland